Penny Stocks: The Next American Gold Rush

Beat Wall Street with the Change in Your Pocket

Dan Holtzclaw

A Publication of Greek Financial Services

Greek Financial Services
5006 Kenton Trace
Suite 21
San Antonio, TX 78240

Cover Design by D. Schroeder,
SDS Designs

First Edition 1999

ISBN 0-9674758-0-5

Contents

Dedication

To my wife, daughter and family.

Acknowledgment

The creation of this book would not have been possible without the hard work and dedication of many individuals. Having said as much, I would like to personally thank the following people who greatly contributed to this text:

To my Father, who scrutinized my ideas and played an instrumental role in shaping this work. This book is immensely improved thanks to his suggestions.

To Julie Farrell, who spent great time and effort editing this book. Her work ensured that this book is easy to comprehend and grammatically correct.

To the thousands of penny stock investors, who spend their valuable time posting messages on the bulletin boards. I refer to their postings regularly for both research and relaxation. Although I have never met many of them in person, I have forged many valuable friendships with posters on the boards. These are the people who make penny stock investing interesting and enjoyable.

Disclaimer

The names of certain stocks, investors, and message board posters have been changed to protect their identity. Any resemblance of these changes to actual stocks or people is purely coincidental. Charts used in this book have been compiled from sources believed to be reliable. The author of this book cannot guarantee the accuracy and timeliness of the information contained in the charts. The author of this book will not be liable to anyone for any misinterpretation, inaccuracy, error, or omission of information in the charts.

The author of this book cannot be held responsible for the actions of individual investors and all investments made by those who read this book are done so on their own merit. The author of this book is not responsible for any losses, monetary or otherwise, incurred by the readers of this book. The author of this book is not and does not make any claim to be a stockbroker, securities analyst, certified financial planner, etc. Any and all trademark rights apply to appropriate companies referenced in this book. The information provided in this book is intended as an adjunct research tool for the aspiring penny stock investor. Investors should rely on other sources of information in addition to this book before making investment decisions. The statements presented in this book are the expressed opinion of the author and should be treated as such. This book makes no solicitation to buy or sell any security that is mentioned within. Investors should fully investigate and understand the risks associated with investing before placing any money into the stock market. Novice investors should consult with a trading professional before making investments.

Preface

Penny stocks…my passion, my love, and the cause of my stomach ulcers! Why did I write this book you might ask? I'll try to give you the short version of how this work came to fruition. I began my stock investing career as most others have by investing in large Dow component stocks that had to be held for long periods of time in order to attain any appreciable results. Being the impatient type, I later jumped on the Nasdaq bandwagon to take advantage of the high flying, fast paced tech sector. I have done well on the Nasdaq and I continue to hold several investments on this exchange. While investing in the big stocks, I would occasionally hear about penny stocks and how some of them could provide a year's salary in just three days if you picked the right one. I must admit that I was quite leery about penny stocks in the past because for all I knew, penny stocks were risky, volatile, and full of scams. I remember the first penny stock that I ever purchased.

It was a Friday and I saw a hot tip while cruising the internet so I took a look at the stock. Within two hours, the stock in question jumped from 50 cents to 65 pennies. I saw this skyward momentum and I put in a market buy order for two thousand shares. That was my first mistake! As you will see later, NEVER place a market order for penny stocks! The stock continued its quick rise, but my order never filled. "What's going on?" I wondered. Why didn't my order fill? The stock kept rising and hit $1.03! Take a guess when the market makers filled my order? You guessed it, $1.03! I couldn't believe it. My order filled at the high and wouldn't you know, as soon as my order filled the price dropped like a rock back down to seventy cents. Fortunately, the price clawed its way back up to 93 cents before the close. My head was swimming with emotions. I was angry. I was nervous. Most of all, however, I was scared...scared that I was about to lose half of the money I had just invested. After the market closed that Friday, I spent the entire weekend agonizing over why I had been so stupid as to purchase that stock. I had no idea how penny stocks operated. I was a Nasdaq investor and was unfamiliar with the rules of the penny game. When Monday rolled around I was blessed by lady luck...or so I thought. The stock opened at a buck and a half. Talk about a gapper! I was ecstatic! I immediately put in a sell order at the market just after the opening, mistake number two. The price began to plummet. I was caught up in a profit-taking sell off and my market order was not getting filled. About thirty minutes into trading the stock hit its low for the day and that is when my order filled. My computer screen flashed a sale at one dollar and fifteen cents. To be honest, I was quite happy to be out of that stock with a profit. My first experience with a penny stock had been a success, well kind of. I checked the quote on that stock at the end of the day and it closed at one dollar and forty-eight cents. My lack of experience in the penny game cost me there.

That experience is one of the reasons why I wanted to write this book. Had anyone ever told me the differences between Dow, Nasdaq and penny stocks, I just might have been able to pull out a larger profit from that first penny investment. Have you ever tried to find a book on penny stocks? I have tried and I can honestly say that I have yet to find one. Most stock investing books do not even mention penny stocks and those that do often treat pennies like they have the plague. The authors of these investment books make comments such as "Penny stocks do not make sense for most investors" and "Investing in penny stocks is much like playing the lotto or going to Vegas". What kind of information is that? There are multitudes of investors out there who have an interest in penny stocks, but there are no books for them to get that information.

Because of this void, new penny investors often have to rely on what they can find on the internet to educate themselves about penny stocks. Searching the internet for penny stock investment data can be difficult and time consuming. The best way to learn about investing in pennies comes from experience. Experience, of course, comes at the expense of time and this is something that the beginning penny investor has yet to sacrifice. So where is a newcomer to the world of penny stock investing to go to get sound and reliable information? Right here! I wrote this book in an effort to solve these problems. I was tired of seeing the "Wizards of Wall Street" ridicule the penny stock community. I was once in a chat room on America Online trying to find some information on penny stocks. I asked if anyone in the room traded penny stocks and you would not believe what happened next. About ten members of the chat room began to call me names and said that penny stocks were a joke. One poster even went so far as to say, "I hate penny stocks and those who invest in them!" When I asked these folks to compare their "big stock portfolios" with my "stupid little penny portfolio" I easily outperformed everyone in the room by at least 50%.

Finally a book is in print which affords the novice penny investor a foundation from which to begin his or her journey into the wonderful world of investing in pennies. This book is not going to tell you which penny stock to pick; that was not my goal in writing this. If I knew which stocks to pick I would be eating dinner with Warren Buffet on a yacht discussing which companies I would like to purchase. I do not have a crystal ball and I cannot predict the next "big winner". I can, however, try to provide you with the tools and information to have a good working knowledge of penny stocks and challenge you to develop a successful strategy so you can be confident in the stocks that you invest in.

1

Introduction

Making money and profits, that is what investing is all about. Traditionally, only those with large bankrolls and access to expensive stockbrokers had the chance to invest in the world of securities trading, leaving the average person out of this exclusive club. However, this is no more. The recent advent of on-line trading has vastly altered the investment landscape. Today anyone with access to a computer has the potential to make money on the stock market. History has seen nothing like this. At no other point in time has the middle class had such opportunity to control the fate of its financial well being.

There are numerous ways to invest one's money depending on the amount of risk one wants to take. Where investing in stocks is concerned, choices abound as there are mutual funds, New York Stock Exchange (NYSE), Nasdaq, and Over-the-Counter-Bulletin-Board (OTCBB) securities to choose from. Of course, the amount of risk taken will determine the possible rewards you will reap. Mutual funds are relatively safe and generally offer around a 10% return on your money. NYSE stocks are the benchmark of securities trading and are the least volatile when compared to Nasdaq and OTCBB stocks.

NYSE and Dow stocks are generally composed of more traditional companies and the prices of the securities on this exchange tend to fluctuate in small increments under normal circumstances. NYSE stocks have provided decent returns over the past decade, but at a much slower pace than the Nasdaq and OTCBB markets. It may take many years for a Dow component to double in value. However, the slow movement of most Dow stocks assures investors that their profits will most likely be safe. By this, I mean that once a Dow stock doubles in value it is not going to give back its gains overnight. If the stock does slide a little, it will occur over an extended period of time thus giving the Dow investor ample opportunity to assess the situation.

While the NYSE tends to be more conventional, the Nasdaq exchange is heavily laden with up and coming industries such as the internet, technology, bio-tech, and communications sectors. The explosive growth of these industries over the past few years has led to phenomenal gains for Nasdaq stocks. While the Nasdaq has handily outperformed the Dow recently, it is a much more volatile exchange and that keeps some investors out. Remember that more profit equates to a higher risk. Some conservative investors avoid the Nasdaq because its stocks do not quite follow the tried and true paths that Dow stocks do. Many Nasdaq companies are not yet profitable and have price to earnings ratios that until recently have been unheard of. A Nasdaq stock can post a loss for a quarter and still be a hot commodity. These situations are confusing to the traditional Dow investor and many will not touch Nasdaq stocks because they fear the new criterion that measure Nasdaq performance. On the flip side the new wave of on-line stock investors seem to like the Nasdaq. Many of the new online investors are of a younger generation and are willing to take higher risks in order to get the type of returns offered by the Nasdaq.

Speaking of great returns, I would be amiss if I forgot to mention the OTCBB market. Stocks on the OTCBB market provide the highest potential for incredible returns on your investment, but they also carry the most risk. Although the OTCBB market is actually regulated by the NASD (National Association of Securities Dealers) who owns the Nasdaq Stock Market, OTCBB stocks are very different than their counterparts on the big boards. Where NYSE and Nasdaq stocks often range in price from just a few dollars to over two hundred dollars per share, OTCBB stocks generally range in price from one hundredth of a cent up to thirty or forty dollars. Both Nasdaq and NYSE stocks are listed in fraction increments such as 36 5/8, whereas OTCBB stocks are listed in decimal format, i.e. 36.625. The decimal format is essential for the OTCBB market because many of its stocks are priced at subpenny and penny levels. Movement on these stocks can often occur in small increments and the use of fractions would just be too confusing for the typical investor. The decimal format on the OTCBB market makes life easier for both the investor and the market maker alike. Because the OTCBB is merely a quotation service for NASD market makers and not an actual securities exchange, bulletin board stocks are not subjected to the stringent rules that the NYSE and Nasdaq stocks are forced to comply with. Up until recently, OTCBB companies were not required to file any sort of information whatsoever. This is one of the reasons bulletin board stocks garnered a "questionable" reputation over the years. The lack of reporting requirements on the OTCBB market led to the unfortunate development of numerous scams. Unscrupulous practices such as "boiler room operations", shell companies, and off shore foreign stocks cost many investors a pretty penny. In an effort to clean up bulletin board stocks, the NASD has recently approved new measures that require all companies to file with the SEC in order to have their quotes posted on the OTCBB network. The NASD amendments to NASD rules 6530 and 6540 to limit quotations on the OTCBB only to those securities of issuers with current reports filed with the SEC or other regulatory agencies. According to the amendment, member firms will be required to inform the NASD of the issuer's reporting schedule. A security of the issuer may continue to be quoted on the OTCBB for a 30 or 60 calendar day grace period following the due date of the report. Stocks that fall into this category will have an "E" added to the end of their stock symbol. The "E" denotes that the security in question is delinquent in their required filings with the SEC. After the grace period has expired, quotations for the stock of the delinquent company will not be permitted on the OTCBB and the stock will most likely move to the pink sheets. The NASD felt that these changes were necessary in order for the investing public to have access to information about the issuers being quoted on the OTCBB. These changes should improve both the safety and reliability of the OTCBB market.

The recent advent of online trading has had the most dramatic impact on the trading of OTCBB securities. In the past, trading bulletin board stocks was difficult and expensive. Prior to the internet obtaining any sort of appreciable intelligence on bulletin board stocks was next to impossible. The only exposure many investors had to OTCBB stocks was from "boiler room operations" that would contact potential customers via telephone and promise incredible returns from unknown stocks. Many of these operations were illegal scams, hence many older investors still have a strong distaste for the OTCBB market. The great expense in trading bulletin board stocks came from the brokers. As the OTCBB was a thinly traded market, brokerage fees were extremely high in relation to the price of the stock. Without these expensive commissions many brokerages probably wouldn't have even offered OTCBB trading. Thankfully, all of that has changed as the internet has revolutionized OTCBB trading in so many ways. Today, information about bulletin board stocks is just a mouse click away. Want to read a company's Securities and Exchange Commission filings? Click on Freedgar.com and read all of their reports free of charge. Want to find the company's address? Click on the company's homepage. Amazing isn't it? These advancements will make investing in penny stocks easier than ever before.

As more investors gain access to online trading, many newcomers will take advantage of trading OTCBB stocks, specifically penny stocks. Investors on the NYSE and Nasdaq consider stocks costing five dollars and under "penny stocks". But we are not talking about those exchanges now are we? We are dealing with the Over-the-Counter Bulletin Board market where a penny stock literally means that the stock costs a penny! As a matter of fact, many bulletin board stocks trade for less than a penny. Just think, you can become a part owner of a company for less than one cent! You probably recognize many of the companies that are found on the penny stock market. Planet Hollywood Restaurants, Levitz Furniture Stores, Zenith, Danskin, Freuhauf Trailers, Golden Bear Golf (Jack Nicklaus' Company), and Eat at Joe's restaurants are just a few of the many well known companies that can be purchased for a few copper pennies.

Penny stocks are attractive to new investors for many reasons. First there is the cost. Many new investors have little capital to invest and penny stocks afford them an opportunity to buy a respectable amount of shares of a security. In addition, there is the unrivaled potential explosiveness of penny stocks. A two cent gain for a stock costing four cents translates into fifty percent profit. Should our new investor with the limited funds invest on the big boards, he may be able to buy just a few shares which must rise considerably in order to provide any type of respectable profit. On the other hand, should our investor stake claim to a few hundred thousand shares of a penny stock, a small jump in price can quickly lead to a nice hefty payday.

Newcomers to the investing game are not the only ones taking advantage of the penny stock bonanza, quite the contrary. More and more seasoned investors are beginning to actively take part in the world of penny stock trading. Now that due diligence, stock research, can be performed on penny stock companies via internet, many investors are seeing that penny stock businesses are real. Additionally, online brokerage firms have made trading penny stocks very affordable, costing as little as $14.95 per trade in some cases. The unbridled capability of penny stocks to achieve stupendous returns is still the main draw of the penny stock. A good friend of mine recently told me that he honestly believes more new millionaires are created on the penny stock market than on both the Dow and Nasdaq combined. To be perfectly honest, I have no doubt that this statement is true. I have seen many penny stocks achieve gains of up to 10,000% in just a few days time. No that is not a typo. A few Nasdaq securities have amassed gains similar to this, but not as frequently as penny stocks have. This is the ultimate goal of penny stock investing, trying to catch that one winning company that will turn your penny investment into a dollar investment.

A prime example of this is seen in a building stock called TNRG. Not too long ago TNRG shares could be purchased for a single penny. Within a few months time, this stock costing a single penny soon was worth one crisp dollar. While a one dollar stock may seem cheap, look at the percent gain that TNRG achieved. One cent moving up to one dollar translates into a 10,000% gain! Had you invested a mere $2,000 in TNRG at its low, you could have sold for $200,000 at the high! Not a bad return for just a few months work. Heck, that's like winning the lottery! This type of success story happens over and over again in the world of penny stocks. EDIG climbed from 13 cents to $22.

XNET began at a quarter and maxed out at 20 bucks. IGHS shot up from 43 cents to just under four bucks. CMOZ raced from 15 cents to over six dollars. I could go on and on with penny stock success stories but I do not want this book getting as thick as an encyclopedia. Almost everyday you can find a penny stock making four digit percentile gains. Do you see this on the Dow and Nasdaq? No way! Well, not in the same time frame.

Now, do not get me wrong, investing in penny stocks has its risks and not everyone who tries their hand at the penny market walks away a winner. As with most other things in life, timing is everything when trading penny stocks. Buy a penny stock near the low and you can become rich should the stock rise. Buy a penny stock near its high and you could get burned should a sell-off occur. Of course these same exact risks apply to the Dow and Nasdaq, but penny stocks take these chances to extreme levels. Penny stocks are very volatile making the risk of the exchanges such as the Dow seem almost nonexistent. Where a Dow stock may take weeks or months to move as little as 5%, penny stocks often fluctuate 5% or more on a daily basis. The volatility of penny stocks is one of their inherent risks. This is why brokerage houses will not allow penny stocks to be purchased on margin; they are just too volatile. You must take the good with the bad. If you don't take the risk you will never have the opportunity to grab the big gains.

So, why are penny stocks the "next American gold rush?" Back in the 1800's, prospecting gold in the hills of California and the mountains of Alaska made many a common man rich beyond his wildest dreams. Today, trading in penny stocks offers the average Joe much the same opportunity. The internet has made penny stock investing both affordable and feasible for the investor with limited resources. No longer will the world of investing be dominated by just a privileged few. Additionally, online discount brokers and the various OTCBB sites and chat rooms have created a newfound interest in penny stocks. Penny stocks have become the antithesis of the big board securities. While it takes a substantial amount of time and money to make it big on the NYSE, trading penny stocks can make you rich overnight. One day gains of 1,000, 2,000, and even 10,000% can and have been made on the penny stock circuit. Do these types of quick gains happen on the larger exchanges? The answer is definitely no and this is one of the main reasons why interest in penny stocks is growing.

Just take a look for yourself; message boards at sites such as Raging Bull are dominated by the penny securities. Check out these numbers from Raging Bull: Amazon (Nasdaq AMZN): 25,000 posts...Microsoft (Nasdaq MSFT): 10,500 posts...IBM (NYSE IBM): 2,942 posts...e.Digital (OTCBB EDIG): 178,700 posts...Pan American BanCorp (OTCBB PABN): 93,000 posts...MPTV (OTCBB MPTV): 73,600 posts...Ameriresource Technologies (OTCBB ARET): 81,000 posts. These numbers show that interest in penny stocks definitely exists and is growing at a rapid pace.

Recent studies show that the OTCBB has 6,667 securities listed, up 7% from 1998. Share volume traded on the OTCBB market was up 136.78% and total dollar volume was up 85.93% from last year as well. This growth is phenomenal and should continue to increase as more and more investors trade penny stocks online. Online discount brokers such as E*Trade and Ameritrade are generating new accounts at a rapid pace and surveys show that many of these accounts are held by new investors with relatively small bankrolls. The inexpensive cost coupled with their explosive potential profitability will make penny stocks a very attractive proposition to these new investors. The new goldrush is upon us and those who miss out will rue the day that they passed on this wonderful opportunity.

2

Frequently Asked Questions

It never fails, whenever I see new faces on the bull boards everyone tends to ask the same questions. There is nothing wrong with asking questions. Remember what your grade school teacher said? No question is a stupid question; the only stupid thing is not asking questions and remaining in the dark. Penny stocks are very different from their big board counterparts. Add to this the fact that it is very hard to find information about trading penny stocks and it is easy to comprehend why new investors are full of questions. The world of over the counter bulletin board trading is very unique because the internet message board plays a very important role in trading. In the following pages are some of the most frequently asked questions seen on the boards along with the information that answers them.

1. Can penny stocks be traded on-line?

Yes they can. The first broker I ever used was very wrong about this. He told me that because penny stocks had such small dollar volume online trading was not available for them. The guy was totally wrong and needless to say he is no longer my broker. Many online trading services such as Webstreet Securities offer OTCBB online trading at very competitive rates. Be sure to shop around before settling on a brokerage to trade penny stocks with. The price of OTCBB trading varies greatly among online brokers ranging from as low as $14.95 a trade up to hundreds of dollars per trade.

2. On the detailed quote, what do bid, ask, last and size mean?

Last – The price of the stock during the last transaction.
Bid – The price at which you can sell the stock.
Ask – The price at which you can purchase the stock.
Last Size – The number of shares involved in the last transaction

3. What are MM's?

MM's are the market makers. These are the guys who actually do the buying and selling of securities. Penny stocks usually have multiple market makers who each have a different bid/ask price. For example, one MM may have an asking price of .042 while another is asking .044. When you place an order for a penny stock the MM's evaluate your offer and decide whether or not to fill it. When dealing with penny stocks, it is the market makers who are responsible for setting the bid/ask price. When penny stocks are doing well investors praise the MM's. When penny stocks tumble investors curse the MM's like there is no tomorrow.

4. What is the "spread"?

The spread is the difference between the bid and the ask price. A stock asking .05 and bidding .045 has a spread of .005 cents. The spread is one aspect that novice penny traders often overlook. After purchasing a stock you must "cover the spread" before you can break even. What does that mean? Well, let's say you buy the stock I just mentioned. You pay .05 cents for the stock but the current bid is only .045. In order to break even you must wait for the bid price to rise up to .05. If this doesn't happen you are going to lose money on your investment. Many novice penny investors only look at the asking price. Before purchasing a penny stock be sure to look at the bid and the ask price. Some penny stocks have enormous percentage differences between the bid and the ask, up to 50% in some cases. Question 15 examines this in greater detail.

5. What does "the float" mean?

The float is the number of shares that a stock has available for trading purposes. The float does not encompass the total number of outstanding shares because some shares are restricted. Company officers or other various parties who may have accepted stock in lieu of cash payments for services rendered often hold restricted shares. Restricted shares have to be held for a specified period of time before they can be sold, hence the term "restricted".

Stocks with small floats can move very quickly during heavy trading activity making it possible for the entire float to be traded in one day. Stocks that have particularly large floats must have enormous trading volume in order for the price to really move. Large floats are also a red flag for reverse splits. This concept is further discussed in question 17.

6. What is "DD"?

DD is due diligence. Basically, the term refers to doing research on a stock. Chapter three contains more information about this topic.

7. What is a pump and dump?

See chapter four.

8. What is a gapper?

See chapter four.

9. What is a shakeout?

See chapter five.

10. What is a wash sale?

Wash sales are a tactic *rumored* to be used by market makers in order to create the illusion of high trading volume. Wash sales work by the market makers repeatedly selling and buying shares from one another at equal prices.

Neither MM actually gains nor loses money on the transaction and the volume increases as a result.

11. How can you tell if the last transaction was a buy or a sell?

If you have access to a ticker on your quote bank, a green (+) indicates that the last transaction was a buy and a red (-) indicates a sale. In the event that you do not have access to a ticker there is still a method for determining if the last transaction was a buy or a sell. Look at the last transaction price. If the price matches the bid then it was a sell. If the price matches the ask then it was a buy. If the last transaction price does not match either the bid or the asking price then it was a limit order that was filled by one of the various market makers.

12. What is the difference between a market and a limit order?

A market order indicates to the market maker that you are willing to buy or sell your security at the current market price. The current market price for a stock changes rapidly and your order may not necessarily fill at the price at which you placed your order. With a limit order you are indicating a price at which you would like to have your order filled. If you place a limit buy order for .05 cents you are telling the MM that you are willing to pay .05 cents or less for that particular stock. If the price rises above your limit then your order will not fill. If you place a limit sell order for .05 cents you are telling the MM that you are willing to sell at .05 cents or higher. If the price drops below your limit the order will not fill. Limit orders offer a degree of protection in comparison to the market order.

Question 16 explains why it is prudent never to place a market order when dealing with penny stocks.

13. Can penny stocks be purchased on margin?

Due to their volatility, brokerage firms shy away from allowing OTCBB stocks to be purchased on margin. This is both a blessing and a curse for the penny investor. The fact that you cannot buy penny stocks on margin does indeed hamper your potential profitability. However, if your penny stock tanks, quickly drops in price, you will be glad that this provision exists.

14. I see many acronyms on the message boards. What do they all mean?

DD – Due Diligence
EOM – End of Message
EPS – Earnings Per Share
FAQ – Frequently Asked Questions
IMHO – In My Humble Opinion
LOL – Laughing Out Loud
MM – Market Maker
MOMO – Momentum Mover
OTCBB – Over the Counter Bulletin Board
P/E – Price to Earnings Ratio
PR – Press Release
ROFLOL – Rolling On Floor Laughing Out Loud
SEC – Securities and Exchange Commission

15. Based on their percentage in relation to the stock, why do penny stocks have such large spreads?

The large spread is due to the fact that penny stocks have low dollar volume. Nasdaq and NYSE stocks have enormous dollar volume in comparison to most OTC stocks. Because of the high dollar volume, MM's can offer smaller spreads on the larger securities and still walk away with a profit. Penny stocks, on the other hand, with their low dollar volume would not be very profitable for the MM's to trade at these same spreads. In order for them to trade OTCBB issues the market makers are forced to open the spread in order to attain the same profitability. When purchasing penny stocks please be very conscientious of the spread. Some penny stocks have spreads that would require a 50% increase in the price of the stock in order to cover the spread; i.e. a stock bidding .01 and asking .015. Many investors would look at this bid/ask thinking that a half-cent rise in the price of the stock is not too great. When investing in stocks, whether it is penny or regular stocks, you must think in terms of percentages rather than actual dollar value. A half-cent rise in a dollar stock is no big deal, but a half-cent rise in a stock worth only one-cent is tremendous.

16. Why is it bad to place a market order for penny stocks?

In nearly all instances placing a market order for penny stocks is very dangerous. "Wait a minute!" you say, "I place market orders for stocks all of the time without any problems." Remember that you are not dealing with regular stocks here, you are dealing in pennies. Penny stocks are heavily controlled by the market makers. When you place a market order you are telling the MM's that you are willing to buy or sell the security in question at the current market price. Unlike limit orders, open market orders afford the investor absolutely no protection from the market makers. Open orders are not filled in the order in which they are received. If a MM receives your market order during a fast paced market he or she may "push your order aside" while they fill limit orders. Meanwhile, as your open market order sits idle, the price of the stock you are trying to buy or sell continues to move. By the time your market order fills the price of the stock may be drastically different from when you originally placed the order.

In a fast paced market this can kill you, remember what happened to my market order in the introduction of this book? In case you forgot I placed the market order at sixty-five cents and it filled at the day's high of $1.03. Had I placed a limit order in that instance I could have saved myself a lot of money. In slow moving markets placing a limit order may be acceptable. However, in my opinion, placing a limit order is the safest way to protect your interests. With a limit order you are the one setting the price, with a market order it is the market makers who set your price.

17. *What is a reverse split? Are they good or bad?*

Just as its name implies, a reverse split is the exact opposite of a normal stock split and is usually an indication that the company is in trouble. Successful companies have normal stock splits due to the fact that the price of their stock has risen to a point that makes it difficult for many investors to purchase shares. By doubling the amount of available shares, the split cuts the price of the stock in half and makes the security more affordable to the average investor. A reverse split acts in the opposite way as it simply "boosts" the price of the company's shares because the stock is failing to rise on its own merit. By reducing the number of available shares by one half, the price of the stock "doubles" in value. The problem with the reverse split is that there is the potential for share dilution. Many times after a reverse split, the company in question will approve the offering of more shares of their stock. Let's say that pre-reverse split you own one hundred thousand shares of a stock costing four cents a share. At this point you own $4000 worth of the stock. If the company has a 1 for 2 reverse split you would then have fifty thousand shares of an eight cent stock. The value of your holdings hasn't changed at all, as you still own $4000 worth of the company. You have not actually lost any money, so what is the problem? The problem is that if the company authorizes more shares, share dilution will occur causing the price of the stock to drop. If the company offers new shares, the price of the stock will undoubtedly fall because the supply of the stock has been increased. An increase in supply without a concurrent increase in demand dictates that the price of the stock will fall. I know that this is a bit confusing, but the end result is that the reverse split in combination with the secondary offering hurts you.

In the past, the reverse split has burned many penny investors and will continue to do so in the future. Stocks with especially large floats are prime candidates for reverse splits. When rumors of the reverse split surface be wary. Do your own investigating, call the company, and decide if the rumors are true. Bashers know that the reverse split strikes terror into the penny investor and they will use that knowledge to their advantage.

18. *Can you get in trouble for making false statements over the internet while posting about stocks?*

Yes you can! Keep this in mind while posting. Each post that you make can be traced back to you through your internet ISP number. This is a special number specifically assigned to your computer when you access the internet. Posts containing false, slanderous, or misleading information may lead to an investigation by the SEC. There have been cases where message board posters have been named in multi-million dollar lawsuits for false and misleading posts. To avoid any problems, only post facts when you are making claims about a company.

A recent example of this was when a new poster came onto one of my boards and claimed that the stock I owned was going to be worthless because the company was filing for chapter eleven bankruptcy protection. I knew for a fact that the company was not doing this so I sent a copy of the slanderous post to both the SEC and the president of the company in question. I informed the poster via bulletin board message that he could get in big trouble for making such unsupported claims and that I had forwarded a copy of his post to the proper authorities. The poster realized the errors of his ways and later made a public apology, admitted that his post was totally false, and asked everyone not to report him. It was too late for this guy. My message had already been sent and I could not take it back. Did he get in trouble? I don't know if he did, but I can tell you that he was very scared after realizing what he had done.

Should you choose to post negative comments on a bulletin board, only post factual data. You can never get into trouble for stating something that can be backed up as truthful. If you see posts that are false or slanderous towards a company forward a copy to the president of the company and use the following link to report the post to the SEC: http://www.sec.gov/enforce/comctr.htm

Please read the story at the end of chapter 9 and then see what you think about posting false messages on the net. Is jailtime and millions of dollars in fines worth posting false rumors? I don't think so!

19. Penny stocks are supposed to have four letter symbols but I see some with five letters. What does this extra letter mean?

A - Class A

B - Class B

C - Issuer qualifications exceptions

D - New

E - Delinquent in required filings with the SEC

F - Foreign

G - First convertible bond

H - Second convertible bond, same company

I - Third convertible bond, same company

J - Voting

K - Nonvoting

L - Miscellaneous situations, such as depository receipts, stubs, additional warrants, and units

M - Fourth preferred, same company

N - Third preferred, same company

O - Second preferred, same company

P - First preferred, same company

Q - Bankruptcy Proceedings

R - Rights

S - Shares of beneficial interest

T - With warrants or with rights

U - Units

V - When issued and when distributed

W - Warrants

Y - ADR (American Depository Receipt)

Z - Miscellaneous situations such as depository receipts, stubs, additional warrants, and units.

20. What exactly is a "penny stock"?

Historically, stocks which trade for less than $5 have been called "penny stocks". For the purposes of this book, a penny stock is considered any stock that trades for less than one dollar. Nearly all penny stocks are traded on the OTC Bulletin Board. As of December 1999, the OTCBB reported that there were approximately 2,800 stocks trading for $1 or less and 3,724 stocks trading for $5 or less.

21. What exactly is the OTCBB?

OTCBB stands for "Over the Counter Bulletin Board". The OTCBB is a realtime quotation service for the National Association of Securities Dealers (NASD) Market Makers. The OTCBB is not an actual exchange in the sense that the New York Stock Exchange and the Nasdaq are. Stock exchanges such as the aforementioned have specific listing standards that bound each security listed. OTCBB securities are considered "unlisted stocks" and until recently were not subjected to any sort of reporting requirements whatsoever. Recent amendments to the Securities Exchange Act of 1934 will require that companies stay current in their SEC filings in order to be listed on the OTCBB quotation service.

22. Who regulates the OTCBB market?

The National Association of Securities Dealers (NASD) regulates the activity of OTCBB market makers. The NASD is a wholly owned subsidiary of the Nasdaq Stock Market, Inc.

23. Can trading be halted on penny stocks?

Yes. The SEC has the authority to halt trading on any OTCBB security including penny stocks.

24. What are Pink Sheets?

The "pink sheets" are a quotation service that competes with the OTCBB for reporting on unlisted securities. Unlike the OTCBB which reports on stocks in realtime over computers, pink sheets report quotes directly to securities brokers via paper on a weekly basis.

25. Which penny stock newsletters and pick sites can I trust?

A good question. There are dozens and dozens of penny pick sites and newsletters on the internet making it difficult to find a good reliable source of information. The best way to gauge whether a site or newsletter is trustworthy is to simply monitor their picks. See what stocks the sites or newsletter recommend and track their performance. You will soon discover which sites are good and which ones are not.

A great new resource for investing in the OTCBB market is the *Microcap Monthly* ezine. This is a brand new "electronic magazine" which focuses on the OTCBB market. Best of all, it is free! By the time this book hits the street, their website should be operational. Pay them a visit at: http://www.microcapmonthly.com

<u>3</u>

Golden Rules of Penny Investing

Rule 1:   **Always perform your own due diligence (DD).**

I cannot stress this enough! When investing you must rely on *yourself* and no one else. Do not trust what you read online at the message boards. Some of the posts may be factual, but many are not. There are hordes of unscrupulous characters floating around the internet and they are known to bend the truth a little. This is the reason every penny stock website has a disclaimer stating that they are not responsible for the posts on their page. The most trustworthy information you will ever find is that which you dig up yourself.

Rule 2:   **Never place a market order when trading penny stocks.**

Do you recall why? If not go back and read question 16 in the "Frequently Asked Questions" section. Basically, a market order places you at the mercy of the market makers. With a market order you have no control over the price at which your stock will move. A limit order on the other hand, puts the control in your hands. With a limit order you are the one dictating the price at which your stock will move. Limit orders may cause you to miss out on a stock in a fast moving run, but the protection they afford is well worth the risk.

Rule 3:   **Ignore the bashers. Ignore the hypsters.**

These posters are examined in greater detail in the Bulletin Board Community section. These types of posters are only out to help themselves. Hypsters make you want to buy a stock and bashers make you want to sell it. That is of course if you actually pay attention to those jokers. More often than not these posters do not have anything of relevance to say. Their posts are sneaky, manipulative and cause confusion on the boards. Ignore what these posters say and rely on your DD.

Rule 4:   **Do not fall in love with one particular penny stock.**

Just because a stock has been good to you in the past does not mean that it will treat you well in the future. After making a nice profit with a particular stock many investors will tend to reinvest in that same stock over and over on the hopes that they will achieve the same success as the first time. This is not a good idea with penny stocks due to the fact that most penny stocks have a refractory period following big gains. By refractory I mean a period of stagnation or even devaluation.

I fell in love with a stock once. I had made a big profit on a certain stock and I knew everything there was to know about the company. As I looked for another company to invest in, I watched the price of my beloved stock tumble. When the stock was down 50% from where I had sold it I thought that it was a good time to jump back in, big mistake. The stock continued to drop and then sat motionless for two months. I finally got fed up and sold taking a 25% loss in the process. Once again I had learned my lesson the hard way. Learn from my mistake. If a stock treats you well take your profits and move on to the next big winner.

Rule 5:   **Don't be afraid to invest in stocks that have burned you in the past.**

Just the opposite of rule four. Just because you lost money on a stock once does not mean that you will lose money the second time around. Perhaps you jumped into the stock at the wrong price on your first try. All stocks can make you money and they can cost you money, it all depends on your timing. Like they say, timing is everything and that is especially true when trading penny stocks. Who knows, maybe on your second dealing with the stock you will make enough profit to cover your losses from the first time you held it. If that happens, you may need to refer back to question four!

Rule 6:   **Constantly Monitor Your Penny Stock Investments.**

The one problem with penny stocks is they are extremely labor intensive. When investing in a penny stock, the burden of researching the company in question rests solely with the individual investor. Unlike stocks on the larger exchanges, there are no brokers to help analyze your penny pick decisions. Once you have finally decided to invest in a particular penny stock, you still have much work ahead of you.

Most penny stocks tend to follow the same pattern. On average, these stocks often sit stagnant or slowly decline on a daily basis. The savior for penny stocks is the "spike." A spike occurs when a stock's value suddenly rises in a short period of time. This quick rise in price generally lasts for only a day or two and then the stock resumes its normal pattern. When the chart for the stock in question is viewed, the quick rise and fall in price creates a "spike." In order to make profits trading penny stocks it is imperative to take advantage of the spikes. Spikes in penny stock value come along on an infrequent basis. Should you fail to sell on the spike, you may have to wait weeks or months before the next spike in price comes along. This is where close scrutiny of your penny stock investment comes into play. A lapse in concentration can cause one to miss the spike, thus prolonging the realization of your profit potential. Therefore, monitor your investments on a daily basis. There would be nothing worse than to find that on the one day you did not watch your investment, your stock spiked and you missed out on the opportunity to sell.

Rule 7: **You cannot lose money on your investment until you sell and likewise, you cannot make money on your investment until you sell.**

So your penny stock is up 50%. Do you have any of that profit in your pocket yet? No you don't because it's still sitting in your brokerage account. This is what we call being rich "on paper". Technically you have the money, but in all actuality the money is not yours until you sell and collect. Let's say you decide to hold out and hope for bigger gains. Oh no! The stock suddenly tanks and your 50% profit rides off into the sunset. The same thing goes for your investments that are at a loss. If you don't sell, you haven't actually lost any money. In theory you could hold those shares forever until they return to the prices at which you bought them. The only problem with this is that by holding your shares you may be missing out on another hot penny play that could provide a much faster return.

Rule 8: **With your long-term investments, hold and buy on the dips.**

This is a simple and easily understandable concept. Dips provide temporary bargain prices for you to add a few more shares to your position. Think of the dips as a sort of "blue light special" on your stock. In addition to being an easy way to accumulate more shares for your long position, buying on the dips also enables you to average down your break-even point. You kill two birds with one stone!

Rule 9:   **Be Wary of Press Releases.**

Press releases can do wonders for a penny stock causing them to double in value in some cases. If you own a penny stock before the PR you will reap the benefits. However, in most cases it is good to avoid buying into a stock following or based on a PR. First of all, buying after the PR usually means that you are going to pay an inflated price for the stock. Second, penny stock PR's are usually forward looking and only contain data that the company wants you to see. Read the SEC10K filing to see what the company is really up to and if you are still interested, buy when the profit taking occurs...it always does

Rule 10:   **Be patient with your investment.**

Penny stocks can sit quiescent for months on end and then shoot up for no apparent reason. Hold any penny stock long enough and you will experience a big day sooner or later. This reminds me of an old Chinese story. Stick with me and you will see how it relates to being patient and having faith in your investment.

A long time ago there was a great emperor who had no heir to his throne. To solve this dilemma the emperor gathered one hundred of the country's finest children and had them visit his royal palace. The great leader addressed the children saying, "One of you will be the next ruler of my kingdom. I have a test for you all and the winner shall assume my position on the throne when I die." The emperor gave each child one seed and instructed

them to plant it in a pot. In one year the children
were to return to the palace to present the emperor
with the results. The great emperor declared that
whoever returned with the grandest tree would win
the throne. The excited children ran home and
eagerly planted the special seeds in their pots. Each
child took exceptional care of his planted seed
giving it plenty of water and sunlight. As the days
turned into months, each child, with the exception
of one little boy, had wonderful tiny trees sprouting
from their earthen jars.   The boy with the treeless
pot was puzzled. Why had his seed not sprouted
like the others? He religiously watered the planted
seed and regularly bathed the pot in a bright stream
of golden sunlight. The child had done everything
right but there was still no tree. The other children
mocked and laughed at the treeless youth.
Nonetheless, the boy kept up his daily regimen and
continued to hope that his tree would one day grow
tall and strong. A year had passed and the children
returned to the royal palace with their trees in tow.
In the back of the room sat the little boy with a
simple pot of dirt. No tree sprouted despite all of
his best efforts. The boy was embarrassed and
feared that the emperor was going to be angry with
him. The great leader addressed the children and
praised them for what a fine job they had done
growing and grooming their foliage. He then said,
"I understand that one of you has a pot with no tree
in it. Would you come forward please?" The boy
in the back of the room was terrified. "What is the
emperor going to do to me?" thought the little child.
The emperor took the boy's treeless pot and gave

him a smile. "This boy, the one with no tree, is the one who shall rule my kingdom when I am gone!" The crowd was dumbfounded. Why had the boy with no tree been chosen as the next ruler of the land? The emperor peered at the room full of children and said, "I gave you each one seed and told you to grow the best tree possible. Each of you has returned with a beautiful tree and this boy brings me a pot of black dirt. Despite your efforts this boy will assume my crown. The reason for this is that I gave you all seeds that had been BOILED! You cheated in your efforts to attain my kingdom. This young boy is the only one who has the patience and honesty to wear my royal crown."

That is a wonderful story isn't it? So, how in the world does that story have anything to do with penny stocks? The little boy in the story had faith in his potted seed. He had done everything that he was supposed to have done and he remained faithful in his efforts despite a lack of results. In the end, the boy with the treeless pot got rewarded for his patience with the entire kingdom. Now pretend that you are that little boy and instead of a seed you have a penny stock. Before buying the stock you did extensive due diligence and undoubtedly felt that this company was a winner. You hold the company for months on end seeing no positive return. As a matter of fact, your investment has actually lost value while you watch other penny stocks riding high. The other investors laugh at you for holding the stock, but you ignore them. Finally the day comes when it's time for your stock to grow. You faithfully held the stock because you did the DD and you knew that you possessed a winner. In the end your stock shoots to the moon and you sell out for a whopping profit. Guess who is laughing now? Patience is a virtue.

A perfect example of a penny stock following the aforementioned story is MVEE. In late 1999, MVEE had dropped to severe subpenny prices, 0.003 to be exact. Of course, the bashers talked about how bad the stock was and how it would soon disappear of the face of the earth. Those who had faith in MVEE continued holding the stock. Lo and behold, in early Jan of 2000, MVEE took off like a rocket! A quick 800% rise up to 0.024 put an end to the bashers' ranting and made a few certain penny investors very happy...not to mention rich as well!

You must realize of course that all stock transactions do not have happy endings. Sometimes you must face the fact that your stock is a stinker and is not going to rise no matter how long you hold it. A problem that is common to both novice and experienced investors alike is holding onto a stock for too long. Everyone has the hope that his or her stock is going to magically rebound and regain its former glory. I'll be the first one to tell you that things don't always work that way. With experience you will learn that sometimes you must sell and take a loss. You can't win them all.

A penny saved is still worth a penny.
A penny invested may turn into many.

- Dan Holtzclaw

4

Picking Winning Pennies

There are over six thousand OTCBB stocks to choose from, so which one do you pick? Choose the right penny and you may become rich, pick the wrong one and you could lose your shirt. How do you decide which stock to buy? When investing in penny stocks you must realize a few things. First of all, take all of the information you know about Dow and Nasdaq stocks and throw it out of the window. Price to earning ratios, debt, assets, quarterly profits, etc...these items do not hold the same merit with penny stocks as they do for securities on the larger exchanges. Additionally, the movements of the Dow and Nasdaq do not bind penny stocks. While the Dow and Nasdaq may drop horrendously on a particular day, penny stocks may often rise. Conversely, there have been many times when the Dow and Nasdaq make terrific gains while most of the major pennies are dropping. Economic factors such as the consumer price index, housing starts, interest rates, etc...also seem to have little effect on the pennies. Rumors, momentum, and future potential are the things that drive penny stock prices.

There are many different ways to invest in penny stocks. Some investments are held for years at a time, while others are held for just a few hours. This chapter deals with due diligence and is meant for those penny stocks which will be held long term. By long term, I am talking about holding a stock for months or years at a time. The long term investment is based on the hope that the company chosen will develop from a small unknown to a major player in its chosen industry.

DD, due diligence, is the art and science of stock research and analysis and is the key to picking winning penny stocks for the long haul. It is the time and effort placed into due diligence that separates the freshman investor from the successful penny mogul. All too often I see posts on the message boards from guys saying that they heard a hot tip and they bought the stock because it was rising. If you take this approach to buying a stock, why not just go and place a bet on tonight's basketball game? You will probably have better odds with the latter. Buying a stock without performing adequate research constitutes gambling, not investing.

Due diligence- how does one go about this important task? Everyone has their own methods for researching and analyzing prospective securities. Some investors simply read a stock's latest press releases, look at the most current quote and consider that adequate scrutiny for justifying their purchase of a stock. On the other hand, I have known guys who have actually visited a company in person to speak with customer relations before they even consider buying into a stock. Which type of due diligence is right, the lackadaisical approach of investor number one or the zealous investigation of investor number two? That is a hard question to answer. The focus of this chapter is to provide an in-depth look at how due diligence can be performed in a fast, successful and efficient manner. At the conclusion of this book, you will find an extensive list of links and web addresses to sites where research on penny stocks can be performed.

Where to Start

Great penny stock investing starts with finding a good broker, because in the world of trading OTCBB securities having the wrong broker can really cost you. Most penny stocks are bought and sold through "discount brokers". Unlike traditional brokerage houses the discount brokers do not offer investment advice to their clients. That is perfectly fine for trading penny stocks because most brokerages do not have analysts covering the OTCBB market. When investing in pennies the burden of researching an investment rests squarely upon the shoulders of the investor. Because most discount brokers do not provide a full range of investment services like the bigger firms they usually offer trades at reduced commission rates.

Through personal experience, I have learned that brokerage firms have great variation in their commission fees for trading OTCBB stocks. Some brokerages charge one simple fee per trade while others charge a trading fee plus a fee for each share traded. Some brokerages have one rate for all types of trades, while others have different commissions based on whether your order is a market, limit, online or touch tone trade. I am sure that most of you reading this book already have a broker with whom you are happy with, but I would like to challenge you to shop around. Are you really getting the best deal possible with your current broker? When I first started trading penny stocks I used the broker that I traded my NYSE and Nasdaq stocks with. While this particular brokerage firm had excellent rates for trading big board securities, they were really terrible when it came to trading OTCBB securities. My first two penny stock trades cost me $164 and $180 in commissions alone! Needless to say I quickly sought out a new broker for my penny stock trades.

How do you go about finding a good penny stock broker? What types of services and commissions should you be looking for? Personally, I feel that a brokerage firm must meet a few specific criteria to be considered acceptable for penny stock trading. Criterion number one: the brokerage firm must allow penny stock trading online. The action in the penny stock market is fast and furious and this makes online trading essential. You can ill afford to waste time on the phone gabbing with your broker while the price of your penny stock is moving. Criterion number two: the brokerage firm should not charge a fee for each share traded. This concept is imperative for making profits in the penny stock market. As penny stocks are very inexpensive your transactions will almost always involve large numbers of shares. Let's say that your broker charges $19.95 plus 2% of the principle traded for an OTCBB transaction. If you were to purchase $3,000 worth of a penny stock your out-of-pocket expense in commission fees is going to be $80 to buy and $80 to sell! After a few trades, those commissions can begin to eat away at your profit margin. Criterion number three: the broker should be easily accessible by phone. This criterion is meant to protect you in those certain situations when you cannot trade online. Perhaps you are on an important business trip and you don't have access to a computer. If you can't reach your broker by phone, how are you going to make any trades? Criterion number four: the brokerage must have competitive rates. This concept needs no explanation.

So now that we have established our criteria how do you go about finding the broker that is right for you? The answer is simple, just ask around. Go to any of the message boards and ask what brokerages other investors are using. I have seen many posters ask questions concerning brokers and their queries are usually answered promptly. Take the leads you obtain from the message boards and investigate them further. Go to the brokerage's website and see what you think. Check out the fee schedule and the website layout. You should find a broker that suits you perfectly in just a matter of hours. Some of the most reliable and inexpensive firms for trading penny stocks online are:

- E*Trade   1-800-ETRADE1
  http://www.etrade.com

- Ameritrade   1-800-669-3900
  http://www.ameritrade.com

- Web Street   1-800-WEBTRADE
  http://www.webstreet.com

- Suretrade   1-401-642-6900
  http://www.suretrade.com

- Waterhouse   1-800-934-4410
  http://www.waterhouse.com

Scanning the Rumor Mills

When searching for a new stock to invest in begin by jumping onto your computer and scanning the rumor mills. Sites such as Bobz.com, Raging Bull, and Silicon Investor all have penny stock message boards where "hot tips" and rumors are posted. Many of the posts on these sites are pure hype and have no merit or value whatsoever, but on occasion you may discover a diamond in the rough. The trick with these posts is knowing how to separate the good posts from the bad and that is where good due diligence comes to play. Use the rumor boards to see which penny stocks are the current darlings of the OTCBB world. Another good source for up and coming penny stocks is the good ol' penny stock newsletter. There are a plethora of penny stock newsletter groups that send out daily penny picks to members of their mailing lists. A word of caution about these penny newsletters: many of these news-groups are composed of individual or multiple investors who publish information about the penny stocks they are currently investing in. The composers of these newsletters may have no official investment training or experience and the newsletter picks may serve the interest of their publishers only. For example, some of the publishers of these newsletters may load up on a stock at cheap prices and subsequently send out their pick after they have acquired a substantial quantity of shares. As the members of their mailing lists rush out to buy the stock picked in the newsletter the publishers sell their shares as the stock begins to rise. In the end, the naïve investor gets stuck with overpriced shares and the newsletter publishers walk away with a pocket full of cash. Of course, not all penny stock newsletters work in this fashion. There are many reputable and respectable newsletter groups out there, but they are hard to find. The reason for this is that almost anyone can start their own mailing list. Who knows, the publisher of the mailing list you're on could be a fifteen-year-old kid! Because it is difficult to find a trustworthy newsletter join every one that you can find. Monitor the results of the newsletter picks over time and see which ones pan out. Add the successful newsletters to your "favorites" list and place the poor ones into the recycle bin.

Some of the best newsletter sites I have found include:

- http://www.Cyberstocks2000.com
- http://www.MicroCapWorld.com
- http://www.hotstocks.com
- http://pennystockgazette.listbot.com
  MRKTcaoch@aol.com
  http://www.marketlegends.com

These sites have proven themselves with multiple winning penny picks and get my seal of approval. A few of the past picks from these sites include:

Stock Pick	Pick Price	High	Time Frame
TSIG	0.04	1.00	1 month
USHO	0.015	0.22	2 weeks
YDSLF	0.75	4.00	1 month
TNRG	0.18	1.05	1 month
ECEC	1.90	21.00	2 weeks
WLGS	0.77	4.25	2-3 weeks

On a normal day, I will receive 20 to 30 emails from various penny news-groups hawking their current penny picks. I use these newsletters in conjunction with the information from the rumor mills as a starting point for my due diligence. From these sources I compile a list of promising and intriguing stocks to further investigate.

In With the Good, Out With the Bad

Having compiled a list of prospective picks from the rumor mills and newsletters, proceed to a general search engine such as Yahoo or Excite to gain a quick overview of the stock in question.

These websites provide a quick look at current quotes, charts, press releases, and company profiles. Use these sites to weed out the stocks that do not interest you. After crossing the unattractive stocks from your list verify that the remaining stocks are members of the "OTCBB Top 100 for volume." I prefer to stay with penny stocks that are on this list because a stock with no volume has little movement. Unless special circumstances exist, any stock not on this list gets crossed off of mine.

All right, your prospective penny list should be getting a little smaller now. To trim your list even further check the 360-day price/volume history for the remaining stocks. Go to the website http://www.dailystocks.com to find detailed price histories and other great information. The volume and price history can be very informative as they can be used to find various trends. In addition, the price/volume history can answer the following questions. Is the stock tanking from a recent run-up? Has the price of the stock sat stagnant for a while? Is the stock at its 52 week low? The stock price history will answer all of these questions and more. Now take a look at the volume history. Has the volume been increasing as of late? Are there any unusual spikes in the volume recently? More importantly, has there been a significant drop in trading volume? If so, what's the cause for the decline? To be successful in your DD you must ask many questions. The easiest way to answer your questions is to simply ask more questions. As you answer one you may find the answer to another. When price and volume are concerned, look for a stock with its price near its 52 week low and with a recent increase in volume. The volume increases can be very subtle, so scrutinize very carefully. The volume increase near the low is often a good indicator that the market makers are quietly accumulating shares at the depressed prices in anticipation of a forthcoming run-up.

Almost There

Having scanned the rumor mills and newsletters, evaluated the quick overview, verified the OTCBB Top 100 list, and examined the price/volume history your prospective stock list should be pretty small at this point. The few stocks that have passed all of these tests have two more challenges remaining before you should consider investing in them. Test number one is the news test. The news test consists of reviewing the company's press releases to see what is going on with the company. News releases must be taken with a grain of salt. Company press releases usually contain "forward looking statements" and only report positive data. It is very rare to see a press release containing negativity. When performing the news test you may be surprised to discover that many penny stock companies are devoid of any press releases. Try to avoid stocks that do not put out press releases. Why? Press releases can do wonders for a penny stock causing them to double in value in some instances. I recently saw a press release that caused a stock to move from 3.4 cents to 4.9 cents within thirty minutes. That's a 44% gain in thirty minutes based solely on the merits of a press release! The stock hit 7 cents at the midday high on the following trading session for a near 100% increase. Would a DOW stock shoot up nearly 100% in less than two days based on a PR? Don't count on it. Why do some press releases send penny stocks through the roof? Dow and Nasdaq stocks have press releases all of the time and unless the news is huge the PR's don't affect the price very much. Penny stocks are a different breed. Remember that most penny stock companies are unknown enterprises that do not have big names like their NYSE and Nasdaq counterparts. A press release gives exposure to a penny stock and can be the spark for a buying frenzy.

I admit that I do buy stocks that have no press releases, but I try to avoid them as much as possible.

The Final Test

Stocks that pass the news test should stay on your list, but they have one more hurdle to clear before you should invest in them. The final, most important, and stringent test for a penny stock is its SEC filings. SEC filings such as the annual 10K report and the quarterly 10QSB reports are cornucopias of information detailing every aspect of the company in question. A company's SEC filings are the safest and most trustworthy source for research when performing your due diligence as they contain absolutely no hype, only facts. Company phone numbers, financial statements, asset analysis, pending lawsuits, company history, and lists of company officers can all be found in the SEC filings. Most SEC filings are very long and boring, but they are essential reading for the serious penny investor. I have mixed feelings about companies who fail to file with the SEC. Without SEC filings, it is difficult to find factual data and you are forced to rely on rumors and unsubstantiated claims as part of your due diligence. Unless the stock seems to be a very hot rumor play, I will almost always avoid stocks that do not file with the SEC. Of course, this point has now become moot since the amendments to NASD rules 6530 and 6540 were put into effect. In case you haven't noticed, SEC filings are my favorite due diligence tool.

By this time, there are usually one or two penny stocks that have passed all of the DD tests. So, is it time to invest yet? Not quite. After your exhaustive research, if you still have lingering questions about the company, do not hesitate to call the company and speak to their investor relations department. Now your due diligence is complete and you can feel comfortable about the company you are about to invest in. Some may say that the DD described in this chapter is excessive, but remember that you are investing your hard-earned money here! Of course, I do not perform such extensive research with all of my penny investments. The strategy outlined in this chapter is what I use for my long-term picks. On these particular picks, I usually invest an abundant amount of money and I want to know exactly what I am getting into. When dealing with gappers, pump & dumps, and others, I often do no DD at all. Since I plan on holding these stocks for only a short period of time, I do not feel that extensive DD is necessary on these plays.

The Quick and Easy Way to Perform DD

A new website has recently opened which, for a small nominal fee, will provide you with the penny stock due diligence that you are looking for. http://www.pennypi.com has gone to great expense to search out, gather, and consolidate independent, credible information on over 6,000 Non-Listed Securities. Most of these companies trade on the OTCBB or in the Pink Sheets. PennyPI does not provide stock picks, that is your job. PennyPI's mission is to is to search the world (online and offline) to find the most accurate information on these allusive Non-Listed Securities. They do not determine whether a company is a good or bad investment. They simply present the facts and let you decide. Give these guys a try.

Due Diligence Summary

- Scan the rumor mills and penny stock newsletters for hot tips and compile a list of prospective penny stocks.

- Use a general search engine such as Yahoo™ or Excite™ to get some general information on the stock. These search engines should provide current quotes, charts, press releases and company profiles. Eliminate those stocks that do not interest you.

- Verify that your prospective investments are members of the "OTCBB 100 Most Active Stocks List." A stock not on this list should be carefully scrutinized before you decide to further pursue it. http://www.otcbb.com

- Check the 360 day price/volume history of the stocks in question. Look for any visible trends or patterns in the volume and pricing. http://www.dailystocks.com

- Examine and analyze the stock's press releases. How often does the company in question put forth news? Does the company have any promising ventures forthcoming?

- Carefully investigate and probe the company's SEC filings. Look for the number of outstanding shares, company debt, assets, pending lawsuits, and anything else you can about the company.

5

Investment Strategies

Planning

Whether you realize it or not, you have a plan for nearly everything you do in life. For example, let's say you are driving your car to the grocery store. First, you will probably make a list of items to purchase at the supermarket. You then get into your car, turn the key and drive away. Take a left on Maple; go through two stoplights; hang a right at Peach Street and pull into the supermarket parking lot. How did you get from your house to the grocery store? You got there by way of a plan. I know that you did not actually sit down and write out everything that you were going to do, but you have probably gone to the supermarket so many times that the plan for buying groceries is firmly implanted in your subconscious psyche. For some strange reason, many investors throw the concept of planning out the window when investing. I can't tell you how many times I've seen guys who blindly jump into a stock, usually at the wrong price I might add, and then have absolutely no idea as to what they plan on doing with it. Many of these guys want to hold their penny stock until it "goes through the roof" or hits the dollar mark. That's no plan; that is a dream! Look at our example of driving to the supermarket. As you drove the car to your destination, you knew exactly how to get there by planning the route you were going to take. Without planning, you would have driven aimlessly around town hoping that by some miracle you would happen to pass by the grocery store. This is exactly how some people treat their investments. They have no plan and they will allow their stock to float haphazardly because they have no clue what they want to do with it. The worst thing you can do is to have no plan at all. Without a plan you are doomed to fail.

Take the case of JB. I met JB on one of the bulletin boards for a stock we had both invested in. We both bought into the stock around 4 cents. I set a goal of selling once we reached twelve cents. I planned on holding the stock for a while and I felt comfortable with my goal. JB, on the other hand, had no plan at all. He wanted to hold onto the stock until it "shot to the moon!" I never knew what he meant by that statement. Did he mean fifty cents, one dollar, one hundred dollars...? As luck would have it our stock had some excellent news, and it reached twelve cents within a few months. As planned, I sold at my target price and walked away with a nice 300% profit. JB continued to hold his shares with dreams of Porsches and Ferraris dancing in his head. The stock peaked at fifteen cents and began to tumble. I sat on the sideline watching the tremendous sell-off. The stock dropped all the way back down to four cents, our original entry point. I was scanning the boards one day and I saw JB posting. I said "hello" and asked him how things were going. JB was not a happy camper. JB never sold any of his holdings during the run up to fifteen cents and now he was moping. I asked JB why he didn't sell when we were over ten cents. JB said that he did not know why he didn't sell, he thought the stock was going to rise forever. JB had no plan and he paid the price. Don't be like JB; set a goal and stick to it. It's the only way to be successful at the penny game.

When you find a stock that you like and you have done sufficient due diligence to satisfy your demands, how do you decide when the best price to buy the stock is? The best thing to do is to set an entry price that you feel comfortable with. If you can catch the stock on a down day, buy on the dip. I can tell you, however, there are certain times when you definitely do not want to get in a stock, especially when investing for the long haul. For long term investments, never buy the stock after a press release. When dealing in penny stocks, a PR almost always provides a temporary boost to the asking price. When the excitement over the announcement dies down the price of the stock usually comes with it. If you bought into the stock during the run-up following the press release you are most likely going to get stuck with some stock that you paid too much for. Of course, this does not happen in all cases. Some PR's are so significant that they send the stock on long term upward surge. In most cases a press release only provides a temporary pop in price.

In addition to press releases, it is also a good idea to avoid penny stocks that have just achieved significant gains. Penny stocks are not like their big board counterparts. Many large cap components have nice charts with a slow and gradual increase in the value of their shares. Most penny stocks act totally different, as they tend to follow what I call the "burst theory". Just take a look at nearly any penny chart and you will see what I am talking about. In the burst theory the price of a penny stock will lie dormant often for months at a time. Then, without warning, BOOM! The price of the stock will skyrocket sometimes for no apparent reason. Given a few days or weeks for reality to set in, the price of the stock usually falls back to earth and the chart ends up with a nice spike. Take a look at the following chart, and you will see what I mean:

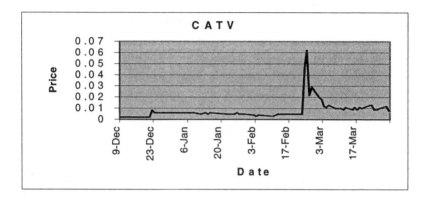

Notice show this stock lay dormant and then spiked tremendously on very heavy trading volume. Out of the blue it traded millions of shares in one day for no apparent reason. More than likely this was a MOMO play. Do you see what I mean by the burst theory? As I was saying earlier, never buy a stock following a recent surge in price, especially if the stock has been sitting stagnant for some time. Had you bought this stock during its huge surge, you could still be holding it at a substantial loss right now. If the stock you want has already spiked either wait and buy when the price comes down or move on to another stock. There is always another winner out there so don't get stuck on one stock. That brings up one other important point. As mentioned in the golden rules of penny trading, don't fall in love with a particular stock.

So, you have bought the stock you want. What are you going to do? When do you plan on selling this stock? You have to decide how much profit you will be happy with. Some folks are happy making ten percent on their investment, while others want much more. Consider the following before making your decision. Do you have a pressing need for your invested money? If so, you probably shouldn't be involved in a long-term investment. Perhaps you will need the money, but not until later down the road. Great, you have a time-line. Set an exit date and get out when you need that money. If you have no pressing need for your invested capital just let it be. Ride out the dips and shakes and wait until your goal is reached. Over time, you must continually reassess and reevaluate your goals. The company you have invested in may have had great earnings in the past quarter or they may recently been named in a terrible lawsuit. As you continue to gather information about the company be sure to modify your goals. You may increase them, lower them, or let them stand pat, but be sure to do something. Goal setting is a dynamic process.

Swing Trades

This is the most common type of investment made on the penny stock market. A swing trade occurs when you buy a stock and hold for a short period of time such as days, weeks, or months. The world of penny stocks seems to run in cycles with certain stocks dominating the scene only to disappear a short time later. After a short hiatus, these same stocks tend to reemerge due to a press release or some other sort of happening. The successful penny investor recognizes these short cycles to see when particular penny stocks are hot. The window of opportunity with these stocks is short and that is why the swing trade is so prevalent with penny stocks. Should you happen to get into a penny stock at the wrong time, you could end up holding it for quite a while until its next run occurs. When performing a swing trade, be on the lookout for clues indicating that the stock in question is on the move. Is the trading volume picking up? Has the bid/ask been increasing as of late? Is the stock mentioned in any newsletters or pick sites? Have you seen the stock mentioned in multiple chat rooms? Are there any rumors abuzz involving this stock? If so, then the stock you are looking at is a good candidate for a swing trade. Companies with expected news such as website openings or pending drug approval are always good for swing trading. The old adage says "buy on the rumor and sell on the news". This statement fits the swing trade like a glove.

Allow me to give an example of one of my recent swing trades. In late April of 1999, I heard a rumor about a company called ARET opening a website. From my past experience, almost every time a company opens a website its stock will surge on the news. I took a look at ARET and performed my usual DD. The company looked good. ARET was one of the top traded OTCBB stocks on a daily basis, it released regular PR's, and most importantly ARET filed regularly with the SEC. I carefully examined the SEC filings and ARET looked like a decent company to invest in especially now that there were website rumors floating all over the internet. I bought a large position in ARET when it was around 2 cents. I held the stock for a few days and news of the website came out. The PR gave a timeline for the opening of the website claiming it would be operational within a month. ARET surged on the news but I continued to hold anticipating bigger gains down the road. Over the next few weeks holding my ARET shares was much like a roller coaster ride. Shakeouts and bashers would drive the price of the stock down and then a PR would come out sending ARET to new highs.

Throughout it all, I continued to hold and buy on the dips. Holding and buying on the dips is not just for long-term penny investments. Swing trades can last for weeks or months providing ample time to use this strategy effectively. By holding and buying on the dips I had nearly doubled my position in ARET in a matter of weeks. As the end of May neared the ARET website had not opened, but I had already made over 200% on my original investment. I continued holding my shares waiting on more news concerning the website. With just a few days remaining in the month, ARET put out a press release stating that the website would be up and running by June 3rd. Excellent! I finally had some news

I could work with. I knew the stock was going to rise over the next few days and I had to decide upon an exit point. When was I going to get out of the stock? Should I wait until the website opens or should I get out before? This was a tough decision. I wanted to maximize my profits but I did not want to get too greedy and get burned by a sell-off. In the end I decided to simply watch the price movement of the stock. I decided that I was going to place a limit sell order for one and a half cents under the current price at the point when I saw weakness in the stock. I planned to place a limit sell order at one and a half cents under the current price to make my offer more attractive to the market makers. After ARET's website announcement the stock took off. We tested the ten cent barrier a few times and as the opening day approached we finally broke through. Two days before the website opened ARET had climbed to around 14 cents. I knew that the day before the website opened was going to be pivotal. Either the stock would fly on anticipation of the opening or it was going to tank in a profit taking sell-off. Personally, I thought why would anyone sell the day before the site opened? Well, on the following day I saw that a sell-off was indeed going to occur. ARET had gapped up in the morning and then large block sells began to flash across my screen. I took this as my sign to get out and I placed a limit sell order for one and a half cents less than the current bid. In the end, I jumped ship making a nice three digit profit in just over a month! Try doing that on the big boards. I'll give you a tip, you can't!

Long Term Investments

This investment strategy is outlined in chapter three, "Picking Winning Pennies". Compared to Dow and Nasdaq stocks, finding a long-term investment in penny stocks is very difficult. The hard fact is that most companies on the penny stock exchange are young and vulnerable. Many of these companies have great concepts and ideas, but they lack that certain something in order to be successful, whether it is efficient management or lack of capital. A true long-term penny investment involves holding the stock for years and requires unparalleled and extensive due diligence on the part of the investor. You must find a company offering a great product or service, a company with remarkable management, and with sufficient capital and resources to carry out its plans. Long-term penny investments are the hardest to find, but they are also the most lucrative. A successful penny investment will become a dollar investment years down the road. Take the case of Starnet Communications (OTCBB: SNMM) a developer, licenser, and provider of online gaming and websites. This company was established in 1995 and has achieved tremendous growth in the past few years. Those who were lucky or smart enough to find this company at its infancy had an opportunity to make unbelievable profits. Just look at this chart:

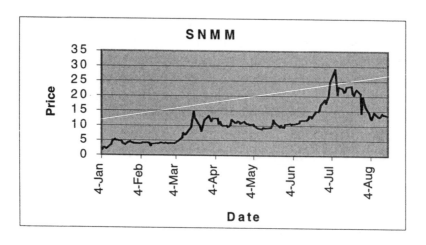

Incredible! This stock once cost less than a dollar and subsequently has risen as high as 27 dollars! That is the beauty of the long-term investment. Find the right company and you can become rich! The trick is finding the right company. When you do find the company you believe is "the one", be sure to remember why you feel that way. You will be holding stock in this company for a long time. Throughout the course of your stock ownership you will undoubtedly experience shakeouts, bashing, stagnation, and so on. The successful penny investors hold and buy on the dips. This strategy is especially true for the long-term penny investment. By holding and adding on the dips, you can significantly increase your position in a stock over time.

A good friend of mine recently had some absolutely amazing success with his long term holds. He told me about these stocks on numerous occasions, but I never did take advantage of his foresight. Big mistake on my part! My pal purchased a few grand worth of YNOT back when it was cheap. He held the stock for a while, some extraordinary developments occurred, and he is now the proud owner of a $20 stock! If you look up YNOT you will not find it...its new symbol is FRLK, or $$$$ as my buddy likes to say. This same friend of mine also purchased IVOC back when it was less than a quarter. He held, the stock took off like a rocket to near $6, and now my friend is planning on purchasing a new Corvette with just a *portion* of his holdings. Wow!

Pump and Dumps

Depending on where you catch it, a pump and dump stock can be a dream come true or your worst nightmare. For those of you who are unaware of the pump and dump allow me to elaborate on this market phenomenon. First of all, pump and dumps seem to focus primarily on the OTCBB sector. While it has been know to occur, pump and dumps do not usually occur on the NYSE and Nasdaq exchanges. The short and sweet definition of a pump and dump is a stock that quickly attains new highs based on hype or unsubstantiated rumors then subsequently falls just as quickly in a profit taking sell off. Play the pump and dump correctly and you can make a pretty penny, no pun intended. Play the pump and dump incorrectly and you run the risk of losing big bucks.

Pump and dump stocks often tend to be obscure securities that usually don't see much trading activity. When a stock is pumped its volume will increase dramatically and the gains in price will be enormous. As the pumped stock begins its climb the hypsters will infect the board like an invading virus. All of a sudden, this stock that was previously ignored like the ugly girl at the prom, is the talk of the town! Everywhere you look hypsters are pumping the stock. How do these guys "pump" you ask? The hypster mixes rumor with fact and focuses on the large gains that the stock has just made. The pumper fails to mention the fact that the stock has had no price movement for three years prior to the pump or that it usually only trades fifty shares a day...how convenient. Classic pump phrases used by the hypsters include such gems as "XYZ is the next EBAY!" and "Triple your money in one day!" The hypster does not provide facts and figures in his posts; only hype and lots of it.

While some pump and dumps only last a few hours others can last for days or weeks. Here is a true story of what some say is a classic pump and dump. The stock STEL was a virtual unknown, sitting at 1.3 cents and a average daily volume of about twenty thousand shares. That translates into $260 worth of trading activity on a daily basis! STEL was a prime target for a pump and dump as a few guys with a couple thousand dollars apiece could easily influence the price of the stock. At the beginning of the pump, STEL's trade volume jumped nearly 1000% to 246,500 shares traded in one day. The actual monetary value of the shares traded that day was still only $3200. STEL closed slightly higher to 1.6 cents on this first day of the pump. Not a huge gain, but this was just the beginning of the pumping phase. When investors saw that STEL had made a nice gain for the day their interest peaked. Combine this with the fact that the hypsters began pumping STEL that night and you had the makings for a classic pump and dump. The following day STEL gapped up to open at 1.8 cents and the frenzy began. Investors flocked to the stock and the price began to climb through the roof! Hypsters pumped STEL like there was no tomorrow. Everywhere you looked there were STEL posts. Someone even claimed that Warren Buffet owned stock in STEL! This stock, that normally traded about twenty thousand shares per day, now had a volume of over five million! STEL closed for the day at ten cents, one dime...a gain of over 500% for the day! With most pump and dump stocks, the day following a huge gain like that would certainly be a dumping day, but STEL was an exception to the rule. On its third day of the pump and dump, STEL continued its amazing run all the way up to an astronomical 68 cents; 68 cents! Just think, if you had invested five thousand dollars in STEL two days ago when it cost 1.3 cents, your holdings were now worth over a quarter of a million dollars! The ride couldn't last forever and as STEL peaked at the high of 68 cents the sell-off began. Profit-takers began dumping their shares and STEL dropped like a rock down to 31 cents. Many who had tried to sell during the dump did not get their orders filled by the market makers. This was probably due to the fact that the price on STEL fell so fast that the limit orders placed by STEL investors became obsolete. That is the problem during the dump. The bid drops so fast during the dump that your limit order can't keep pace. Unless you had placed a limit sell order well below the current bid, the price will probably drop below your limit before the order fills. Now you are in trouble! Over the next few days the dump on STEL continued and the volume began to tail off. At the time when this book was being written, STEL sat at six cents and has regained its normal volume of about twenty thousand shares per day. Here is the chart:

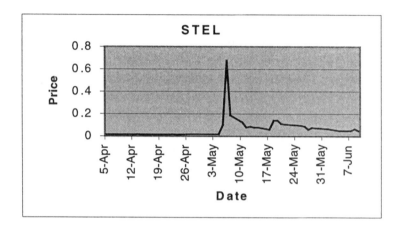

STEL was pumped and then it was dumped. Even though it may be a great company, the bad thing for STEL is that investors now associate it with other pump and dump stocks. Once a stock has been through a pump and dump penny investors tend to avoid it. STEL made a lot of people rich and it also cost many investors the shirt off of their back. Where a pump and dump is concerned everything depends on the timing.

I harbor no bad feelings toward pump and dumps. I have been on both sides of the P&D equation making huge profits on the pumps and losing just as much on the dumps. When you spot a pump and dump stock approach it with caution. Play pump and dumps for a quick buck. No long term investment here. After purchasing a P&D stock set a price goal for selling rather than holding until the price tops out. If you buy a pump and dump stock at seven cents set a goal to sell at a price you feel comfortable with no matter what happens. With this strategy you assure yourself a nice profit...that is, of course, provided that the stock actually runs up to your goal. It is always best to sell a stock while it is on the way up. Selling during the upward pump ensures that there will be a plethora of potential buyers. You should have no problem selling a stock while its price is still on the rise. The problem begins when the dump occurs. Trying to sell during the dump is like trying to sell ice to Eskimos. During a dump you are trying to sell a stock that is out of demand; everyone is selling and no one is buying. Hence, the reason for the tremendous flop in price during the dump. If you have the fortitude to play the pump and dump you must avoid the dump at all costs. By selling on the upside you are guaranteed to miss the dump. There have been many times when I sold out too early and missed out on some bigger profits. I did, however, miss the dump and that is what is important. Remember that you should never feel bad about taking a profit. If you decide to try your hand at the pump and dump you must set goals and sell on the upside. Occasionally, your goal may not be met and you will get caught in the dump. You can't win them all. Use those experiences to adjust your goal setting for the next P&D. Pump and dumps are not for everyone, as they are extremely risky. The secret to pump and dumps is all in the timing.

Gappers

One of the easiest surefire ways to walk away from a stock with a profit is to take advantage of the "gapper". First of all, let me make this clear: gappers can go either way, up or down. This chapter focuses on the upside gappers and how to take advantage of them. So, what is a gapper? The difference in the price of a stock from when it closes to when it opens is called the "gap". For example, let's say that a stock closes for the day at .043. If the stock opens on the following day at .048 an upward gap of .005 has occurred. Got it? Good! Gappers tend to happen following days when a stock has a particularly good day or when news is released after the closing bell. On days following big gains the market makers will often open the stock at a higher bid/ask on the hope that demand for the stock will spill over from the previous day. Many times when a gapper occurs, profit-taking sell-offs will follow. These sell-offs aren't usually huge, but they are big enough to cause a slight dip in the price of the stock. To ensure that you will make a profit from playing the gap sell immediately at the open. On numerous occasions I have seen stocks gap up at the open, rise for about thirty minutes, and then fall in profit-taking sell-offs to levels below the opening price. You must act quickly to take advantage of the gapper. If you get greedy and wait too long to sell you will get caught in the profit-taking sell-off. To protect yourself from the sell-off place a limit sell order at the open. Once you have sold on the gapper, be patient and wait for the profit taking to begin. When the sell-off happens use the dip in price as a buying opportunity if you plan on jumping back into that stock.

If you are looking to play a stock for a gapper, search for a penny stock that is having a great day with big gains and huge volume. Buy a position in the stock just before the market close. Remember this: in order to be in position to play the gap, you must own the stock before the close. If a gapper occurs with the stock that you purchased sell immediately at the open and take your profits. If no gap up occurs keep your eye on the stock and watch the price movement. A stock that doesn't gap up following a day of big gains is usually going to tank, but this is not true in all cases. Some penny stocks can go many days in a row with great gains. Gapper plays are not long-term investments and are often held for less than twenty-four hours.

An example of an OTCBB gapper I played was Global Telephone Communications. While scanning the rumor mills as I usually tend to do I was alerted to a OTCBB stock that was making some unusual moves. For no reason in particular Global Telephone was in the midst of a nice run by the midpoint of the trading day. There was no news, no hype, nothing. Global

Telephone just seemed to be climbing on momentum alone. I took a look at the stock and I bought in about one hour before the close. Global Telephone closed for the day slightly higher than what I paid for it. I wasn't too concerned about the close. I was focusing on the next day's open. Would I get a gapper? I sure hoped so. As luck would have it, Global Telephone gapped up nicely at the next opening. I sold as soon as the morning bell rang and walked away with a nice little profit. Not bad for only holding the stock overnight! Now don't get me wrong, I don't win all of the gappers that I play. But like the saying goes, you can't win if you don't play the game.

Gappers can occur with all stocks, even the ones that you hold long term. If one of your long stocks gaps up should you sell to take advantage of the gap and repurchase on the dip? My answer to this is no, but many people do this and do it successfully. Personally, I do not play the gaps on stocks that I am holding long-term. When a gap occurs on my long stocks I simply hold and ride out whatever happens. Much like the pump and dump, playing the gaps is not for everyone. You must have nerves of steel and be prepared to take a loss if things don't work out. When you play the gap correctly you can take home a quick little profit.

The Shotgun Approach

This is probably one of the riskiest approaches to investing in penny stocks. How does it work? With the shotgun approach you spread your investment out to multiple penny companies hoping that one of them will pay off. It is sort of the same concept that mutual funds are based on. Let's say that you have five thousand dollars to invest using the shotgun method. Divide that money into five one thousand dollar blocks and invest in five different penny companies. Since you are only investing one thousand dollars in each company it would behoove you to invest in the cheapest stocks you can find. This way you can get the most shares for your buck. I like to call this "bottom feeding" as you are looking for the stocks that are at the bottom of the penny stock price range. The concept behind the shotgun approach is that you are hoping for at least one of your picks to take off. Generally, since you will be investing in inexpensive little known companies, the stocks you buy will probably sit dormant for quite a while. So long as you don't sell, you will not lose money and you will not make money. The risk involved with the shotgun approach occurs because these stocks are so inexpensive they usually have large spreads. This concept of large penny stock spreads was covered in question 15 of the FAQ section. If the stocks in your shotgun portfolio never rise you will have to sell them at the ask and this often means losing up to 50% of your investment in that particular security. With the shotgun method you are hoping for one of your stocks to breakout as the stock in the following chart did.

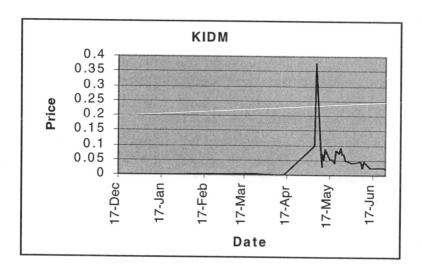

KIDM was a very inexpensive stock for months on end and then BANG! The stock broke out and shot up to over a quarter in one day. I remember this stock well. I checked the quote on the day it broke out and its one-day gain was 9000%! No, that is not a typo. Just for grins, I grabbed my calculator and figured out that if you had invested five thousand dollars at the day's low, your investment would have been worth nearly half a million dollars at the end of the day! Incredible isn't it? You could almost retire on one day's investment! This scenario is the ultimate goal of the shotgun approach. Should one of your picks make this type of move you will do well. Should two or three of your picks do this you could become a very rich person! The shotgun approach would make any serious Wall-Street investor cringe. This method of investing is almost equal to gambling because the stocks at this level of investing usually do not have any type of information for you to do DD on them.

While the shotgun approach does have the potential for big gains it does have a few drawbacks to consider. First of all, to set up a shotgun portfolio multiple stocks must be purchased which means multiple brokerage fees for each transaction. Depending on the cost of your broker this could turn into an expensive proposition. Secondly, this investing approach is very time consuming, as each stock in the shotgun portfolio must be closely monitored for any unusual movement. Because of the type of stocks chosen for the shotgun method, any jump in price must be taken advantage of. If you overlook these scarce spikes in price you may be holding the stock for quite a while until the next pop comes along. If you choose to accept these risks the shotgun approach may be right up your alley. Personally, I would not use this approach as my only investment, but if you have a little spare change lying around...

It just so happened that I was discussing this method of investing with an associate one weekend and he was very intrigued. I explained the basic principles of the shotgun approach and he was sold on the idea. I told my pal that we would create a shotgun portfolio together. To compile our "shotgun portfolio" my friend and I began scouring the internet for penny stocks which were both inexpensive and thinly traded. We wanted thinly traded stocks in our portfolio because any significant events such as a press release could cause a spike in both volume and price. We examined the OTCBB top 100 list, rumor sites, and newsletters for potential picks. After some exhaustive research we finally settled on CHUR, AREE, SNTS, PABN, and CODD. Each of these stocks cost under two cents and some of them were thinly traded. With said portfolio, I was curious to see how things were going to pan out. I felt that each of the companies we chose had potential and could easily double or triple in value with any sort of good news. To be honest, I would have been happy if just one of our chosen stocks received a pop in price.

As expected, the stocks we picked sat relatively quiescent for the first few weeks. Although there was little movement up, there was also little movement down so we were sitting at level par. Then it happened, our shotgun stocks began to fire on all cylinders. First it was PABN. With a flurry of press releases PABN began an incredible run. We held for the ride and dumped our holdings at sixteen cents for an amazing gain. We did it! As far as I was concerned our shotgun portfolio was a success. Even if none of the other stocks achieved any gains we could still drop our position and walk away with a nice profit. I really did not expect any of the remaining stocks in our shotgun portfolio to move, but once again I was wrong. Shortly after PABN's run CODD made its move. I could not believe what I was seeing! CODD made an unexpected quick run and we got out at ten cents. Incredible! Our portfolio had two big winners now after a few short months. To say the least, I was ecstatic with our results thus far. We had made great gains with two of our five picks, but I expected our remaining stocks to sit stagnant and I didn't really care what happened to them. Fortunately, our little shotgun stocks were ready to prove me wrong yet again. A short while after the PABN and CODD affairs all of our remaining stocks made nice moves and we jumped on the spikes. Although our remaining stocks did not achieve the same prosperity as our two big winners, they each made gains of at least 100%. Imagine that! Our worst performing stocks had gains of over 100%! Try finding those kinds of results with a run of the mill mutual fund. In the end our shotgun portfolio was successful beyond my wildest dreams. Below is a table of the results from that legendary play:

Stock	Starting Price	End Price	%Gain
CHUR	0.013	0.028	115%
AREE	0.014	0.042	200%
SNTS	0.011	0.027	145%
PABN	0.018	0.16	788%
CODD	0.014	0.10	614%
Net Gain:			1862%

Can you believe it? Our little shotgun investment came to fruition and netted over 1800% in just a few short months! Realize of course that this type of performance is extremely unusual and I don't expect to see anything like this ever again. However, I could be wrong. Penny stocks make extraordinary gains everyday and it is possible to achieve even greater results with a little luck and patience. If you pick the right pennies there is no telling how high your portfolio can fly!

MOMO Plays

MOMO plays, otherwise known as "momentum movers," are another type of penny stock investment. The MOMO play is a stock pick that is given by investment clubs to members of their mailing lists. MOMO plays usually focus on little known penny stocks that normally have very minor trading volume. When the MOMO play is announced to the public the picked stock will move like wildfire. I have seen instances where a MOMO pick has tripled in value within fifteen minutes of its release. The volume on these stocks will be virtually nonexistent until the MOMO pick is given. Following the release of the MOMO play, there is an immense surge in trading volume and the price of the stock may double or triple within minutes. Look at the chart below:

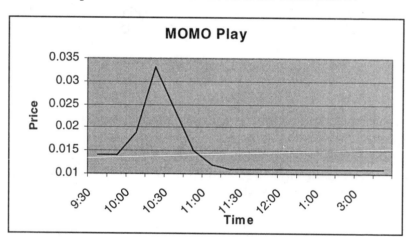

This MOMO pick was released at 9:45 AM. Notice how the price and volume stay fairly level until the time at which the pick is released. Following the release, both the price and the volume take off like a banshee. The problem with MOMO plays is that they move very quickly and you never know when the price is going to tumble with profit taking. Because the MOMO plays move so fast, a limit order is simply out of the question. MOMO's almost always have to be played with market orders if you want to get in. MOMO's move so quickly that limit orders often become obsolete as the price rockets upwards. You can place a limit order on these MOMO plays, but there is no guarantee that it will be filled. A market order will definitely get filled, but the question is at what price will it fill? MOMO plays are meant to last just a few minutes to a few hours. If you get in at the wrong point you could be left holding a bunch of overpriced toilet paper following the profit taking sell-off.

Take a look at this example. A stock investing club emailed me a MOMO pick at 9:45 AM and the darn stock was already tanking by 10:20 AM. By 11:15 AM the stock was down 25% from where it opened. If I had placed an order for this stock when the MOMO pick was emailed to me, I would have been up the creek without a paddle by the time my order filled! Can you imagine? My order would most likely have been filled at the high and I would have lost my shirt in the ensuing sell-off. At the end of the trading day I received another email from that very same investing club boasting about how their MOMO pick was such a "great success." The email read, "The X Group is happy to announce that today's MOMO pick was a whopping success! Price at the time of release was .015 and the stock hit an intraday high over .030 for a 100%+ gain! Congratulations to all who took advantage of this monster pick...". Can you believe the nerve of these guys? Their little MOMO play had a thirty-minute spike in price and they think that they are God's gift to the stock world. I'd be willing to bet the farm that the only people who made a profit on this MOMO play was the club who actually released the pick.

In my experience with penny stocks I have seen the MOMO play burn many investors. Therefore, I avoid them all together. While they may be legitimate, I do not trust the folks

who publish the MOMO plays. Let me give you an example of why I feel these MOMO guys are suspicious. I got an email from a group touting its MOMO play for the day. I watched the MOMO stock curiously and was amazed at what I saw. As usual, the MOMO pick shot through the roof minutes after the pick was emailed to the public. After the price had risen about 100% a huge profit-taking sell-off began. Huge block trades encompassing hundreds of thousands of shares were dumped like crates of tea at the Boston Tea Party. The MOMO pick tumbled and actually finished down for the day and many investors were burned as they got stuck with shares of the worthless stock. As is often the case, the price plummeted so quickly that they were unable to get rid of their shares during the sell-off. I have a sneaky suspicion that the guys who release these MOMO picks accumulate shares before the pick is released and then dump these same shares during the run-up after the pick is given. While the MOMO pickers are selling their shares for profit the average Joe is buying up the very same stock at inflated prices. Following this MOMO fiasco, investors were furious and they began bashing the investment club that emailed the pick. In its defense, the stock picking club sent out emails claiming that a rival group had hacked into their computers and secretly acquired their MOMO picks a few days in advance. It was claimed that this rival group bought up large amounts of the stock before the pick was released and then dumped them during the run-up. The share dumping caused the MOMO pick to tumble and once again the average Joe was burned to a crisp. The story sounded fishy to me and reaffirmed my conviction to avoid the MOMO play. I am not saying that all MOMO plays are scams. I am sure that some of the MOMO picking clubs are legitimate and respectable operations. However, I have seen too many people lose in the MOMO play and I will not risk my money there.
To be fair to the MOMO play, I must say that it does work on occasion. Although I tend to avoid MOMO plays, I have many

associates who regularly invest in these volatile opportunities. Penny stock investors take the highest risk of all investors in the market and those who invest in the MOMO's take these risks to the highest extreme. Because the MOMO is so precarious, the rewards must be great. This is the lure of the MOMO play and this is why my associates try their hand at this play. A good friend of mine just finished a successful MOMO play with a stock called YESS.

My pal had been alerted to YESS by a small investment club that he belonged to. Apparently the club had gained information that YES! Entertainment (YESS) was going to strike some sort of deal with the World Wrestling Federation (WWF). Yes, a marketing deal between YESS and the television melodrama of big muscle-bound men in tights had the potential to send this stock through the roof. My buddy received a MOMO tip on YESS when it was at 15 cents. By the time his order had filled, YESS was at 17 cents. My buddy emailed me this MOMO play when it was at 17 cents, but when I logged into my brokerage account, the asking price had already shot up to 29 cents. Since YESS had already achieved a near 100% gain at that point, I decided not to jump into the stock. Why not? I have been burned by purchasing stocks after they have had big runs and I felt that some profit taking on YESS was eminent. YESS closed for the day at over 30 cents, achieving a 100% gain. Not too bad for a MOMO play. My buddy held the stock overnight hoping for a gapper. Boy did he get it! YESS gapped up to 40 cents the next morning and my associate sold out for a nice profit. His MOMO/gapper play netted him a big payday. Now that I think about it, this stock would have been perfect for a gapper play. It had gone up 100% for the day and closed on an uptick; this was a prime gapping opportunity. Oh well, hindsight is always 20/20. If I did everything right I would be richer than Bill Gates right now. But alas, this is obviously not the case.

MOMO plays can be very enticing. A 100% gain in just a few minutes or hours. Some DOW stocks can take years to achieve that kind of return! With the potential rewards comes the reality of risk. Do you want to take the gamble of losing on the MOMO play in order to achieve those big gains? You know how I feel about the MOMO, but I have many friends who make (and lose) a lot of money on these plays. The choice is yours.

Averaging Down

Simply put, averaging down is a way to make the best out of a bad situation. Let's say that you have the misfortune of purchasing a stock that tanks right after you buy it. Penny stocks do this quite frequently so be prepared. What do you do in this situation? You could sell, take your loss and move on to the next "big winner," or you could sit tight and wait passively as you hope for the price of your stock to rise from the ashes. Those two options don't sound too appealing, do they? Why not take a proactive approach to this situation and average down on the stock? The concept of averaging down is simple: buy the same stock at two different prices, take the average of those two prices and that is your new break even point. Got it?

Here is an example of how averaging down works. You buy a stock at ten cents and it subsequently suffers a horrendous set back falling to six cents. If you sell, you will incur a 40% loss on your investment. If you hold, there is no way of knowing how long it will take for the stock to regain its former glory at ten cents. By holding the stock for an extended period of time, as you hope to get back to even, there will be a multitude of opportunities passing you by. You will miss out on these opportunities because your money will be tied up in that loser stock you own.   In the end, you decide to take the bull by the horns and average down. To do so, you buy shares of the same stock that you currently own at the temporarily deflated prices. Now you have two blocks of stock, one purchased at ten cents and one purchased at six cents. Average the two groups of stocks together and you have now paid an average of only eight cents for your holdings. Your new break even point is eight cents, 20% lower than the ten cent mark you previously sat at.

Averaging down sounds simple and effective, but what are the pros and cons? The risky part to averaging down is that you are effectively increasing the amount of capital that you have tied up in a particular security. If the stock fails to rebound from its slide you could end up losing quite a bit more than you had originally invested. In addition, to average down you must have some reserve capital left at your disposal. If you have stuck your entire bankroll into the market, averaging down is out of the question. Now, assuming you do have money left to average down, what are the benefits? We have already discussed how averaging down reduces your break even point. Should your stock rise from the dead, averaging down essentially turns your old break even mark to a point where a nice profit can be obtained. In our example you originally bought the stock at ten cents and later averaged down to eight cents. Let's say that your stock has a favorable press release and makes a move, climbing from six cents all the way back to ten cents. Wow, a 40% gain! Must have been a great press release! So the stock makes its way back to ten cents. Had you not averaged down you could sell now and basically break even minus the commission fees for trading the stock. But we did average down, remember? Your averaged down break even point was changed to eight cents. If you sell at ten cents, you take home a nice respectable profit. Holding allowed you to break even while averaging down put money in your pocket. Don't get me wrong, averaging down does not work every time. Losses can and will be incurred with averaging down, but the potential for turning a losing situation into a winning situation is enough to offset these risks.

Trend Trades

As mentioned in chapter four, many penny stocks tend to fall into a pattern over time. The investor who recognizes these patterns can use them to his or her advantage and walk away with a tremendous profit. Trends may be difficult to recognize for the beginning penny investor, but as you gain more experience, your skills will sharpen allowing you to easily discern abnormalities in a stock's trading activity.

Finding trends is not an easy thing to do as it takes a lot time and effort on the part of the investor. It is best to have some sort of knowledge about the company that you are following before you decide to invest. Technically, the trend trade can be considered a swing trade. The concept of a trend trade is to buy a penny stock when it is at the start of a new pattern cycle and to sell it when it reaches the end of the identified historical pattern. For example, say you discover that whenever a particular stock hits four cents it usually rebounds to a nickel within a few weeks. The four cent low is what you would call a support point. The support point is that price at which a stock tends to bottom out at before returning to higher levels. In this example, the five cent mark is at the peak of the cycle and is what you would call your resistance or selling point. To successfully identify a stock trend you must identify both the support point and the selling point. When you have identified these prices the next logical step is to wait for your stock to hit the established support price before buying. If the pattern you have identified holds true, you should sell out at the predetermined selling point. To show you how this would work in real life situations, let's take a look at a few penny stocks that have demonstrated trends in the past:

Example # 1: ARET

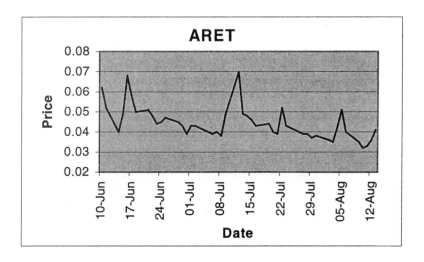

Printed above is a one month price and volume chart of ARET. Look closely at the one month price history for this stock. Do you see a pattern emerging? Can you identify the support point and the resistance point? Notice how this stock seems to bottom out in the mid to high three cent range. When ARET's cycle began, it initially popped up to around seven cents. After hitting its selling point, ARET once again dropped to the three cent range and hit its resistance point. ARET shares subsequently rebounded to near seven cents in a second cycle. We have identified that this stock is falling into a pattern. It is hitting a support level in the mid to high three cent range and is maxing out between five and six cents on average before dropping again. If you felt comfortable with this pattern the logical thing to do would be to buy this stock the next time it was in the mid to high three cent range. If the pattern holds true to form ARET should rise above five cents within a few weeks. A good selling point for this particular pattern play might be 5.2 to 5.4 cents. Playing the pattern on this particular stock would give you a nice 25% gain if the trend holds true. Realize, however, that these patterns are ever changing and may not perform the way you expect. If things were as easy as they seem we would all be rich now wouldn't we?

Example #2: TSIG

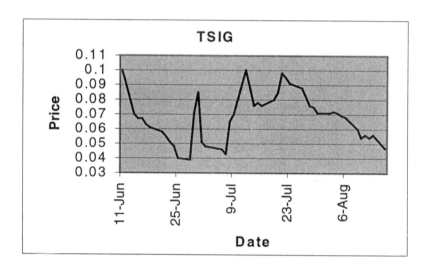

Printed above is a two month price and volume chart for the penny stock TSIG. Once again, look at this chart closely and see if you can find a trend emerging. What did you see? Notice how TSIG hits a support point around five cents. The stock rose sharply to around nine cents and then tanked to nickel levels once more. After sitting around five cents for about a week, TSIG started its cycle again rising to approximately a dime this time. We have now identified the support and selling points here.

TSIG's current support point appears to be in the five cent range. Should you decide to do a trend play with this stock, the logical thing to do would be to wait patiently until TSIG once again falls into the five cent range before buying. IF TSIG never falls back to five cents just keep watching it to see if a new pattern emerges. Should you get lucky and find TSIG available at your predetermined support point, a good selling point might be somewhere just above nine cents *if* the pattern for this stock holds true.

UPDATE: At the time of the second printing of this book, TSIG was on major run and achieved new highs up to $1! Not a bad gain for identifying the support point at 5 cents!

Example #3: FONX

In this example, rather than using a chart, I have used the actual daily price history of this stock to demonstrate its pattern. I prefer to use the actual daily price history over charts because the price history allows you to better determine the support levels for the stock. I understand that all these numbers may look overwhelming, but this is what you have to deal with when trying to spot trends in the daily price sheet. In the following chart, the trends have been underlined:

Date	close/open/high		Date	close/open/high
1/24/2000	.420 .277 .470		1/25/2000	.535 .50 .60
1/21/2000	.245 .247 .247		1/20/2000	.247 .245 .250
1/19/2000	.250 .252 .252		1/18/2000	.252 .254 .265
1/14/2000	.255 .259 .259		1/13/2000	.255 .255 .255
1/12/2000	.255 .260 .260		1/11/2000	.260 .272 .275
1/10/2000	.269 .270 .273		1/07/2000	.270 .275 .277
1/06/2000	.275 .277 .281		1/05/2000	.280 .282 .282
1/04/2000	.276 .295 .295		1/03/2000	.285 .300 .320

12/31/1999	.290	.285	.312	12/30/1999	.280	.280	.290

12/31/1999 .290 .285 .312 12/30/1999 .280 .280 .290
12/29/1999 .280 .290 .300 12/28/1999 .280 .300 .305
12/27/1999 .300 .312 .320 12/23/1999 .312 .325 .325
12/22/1999 .325 .310 .325 12/21/1999 .320 .310 .330
12/20/1999 .320 .400 .400 12/17/1999 .400 .402 .410
12/16/1999 .400 .400 .430 12/15/1999 .400 .375 .400
12/14/1999 .375 .370 .380 12/13/1999 .360 .305 .380
12/10/1999 .330 .315 .330 12/09/1999 .315 .312 .315
12/08/1999 .312 .320 .320 12/07/1999 .300 .330 .340
12/03/1999 .469 .469 .469 12/02/1999 .469 .500 .500
12/01/1999 .500 .500 .531 11/30/1999 .500 .563 .563
11/29/1999 .500 .719 1.000 11/26/1999 .406 .438 .438
11/24/1999 .406 .469 .594 11/23/1999 .313 .313 .344
11/22/1999 .313 .375 .375 11/19/1999 .375 .406 .406
11/18/1999 .375 .375 .406 11/17/1999 .375 .406 .406
11/16/1999 .375 .375 .406 11/15/1999 .375 .375 .406
11/12/1999 .375 .406 .406 11/11/1999 .406 .375 .406
11/10/1999 .375 .375 .406 11/09/1999 .406 .438 .438
11/08/1999 .406 .438 .438 11/05/1999 .438 .406 .469
11/04/1999 .406 .500 .500 11/03/1999 .469 .531 .531
11/02/1999 .531 .563 .563 11/01/1999 .531 .531 .594
10/29/1999 .531 .594 .625 10/28/1999 .594 .719 .719
10/27/1999 .656 .719 .781 10/26/1999 .625 .469 .625
10/25/1999 .438 .500 .531 10/22/1999 .531 .781 .781
10/21/1999 .688 .469 .781 10/20/1999 .438 .375 .438
10/19/1999 .313 .281 .313 10/18/1999 .281 .281 .281
10/15/1999 .281 .281 .313 10/14/1999 .281 .281 .313
10/13/1999 .313 .313 .313 10/12/1999 .313 .313 .344
10/11/1999 .313 .344 .344 10/08/1999 .313 .313 .344
10/07/1999 .313 .344 .344 10/06/1999 .344 .344 .344
10/05/1999 .344 .313 .344 10/04/1999 .313 .344 .344
10/01/1999 .313 .344 .375 9/30/1999 .375 .344 .375
9/29/1999 .313 .344 .344 9/28/1999 .344 .313 .344
9/27/1999 .313 .313 .313 9/24/1999 .281 .281 .313
9/23/1999 .313 .313 .313 9/22/1999 .313 .344 .344
9/21/1999 .313 .313 .344 9/20/1999 .313 .344 .375
9/17/1999 .375 .438 .438 9/16/1999 .406 .406 .500
9/15/1999 .313 .313 .344 9/14/1999 .313 .281 .344
9/13/1999 .281 .281 .313 9/10/1999 .313 .344 .344
9/09/1999 .344 .344 .375 9/08/1999 .344 .375 .406

9/07/1999 .375 .438 .438   9/03/1999 .406 .438 .500
9/02/1999 .375 .406 .438   9/01/1999 .406 .438 .469
8/31/1999 .438 .469 .469   8/30/1999 .469 .531 .531
8/27/1999 .500 .531 .563   8/26/1999 .531 .594 .594
8/25/1999 .563 .594 .594   8/24/1999 .563 .531 .594
8/23/1999 .531 .563 .594   8/20/1999 .563 .531 .563
8/19/1999 .531 .563 .594   8/18/1999 .563 .625 .625
8/17/1999 .625 .625 .656   8/16/1999 .625 .625 .719
8/13/1999 .688 .781 .813   8/12/1999 .813 .688 .875
8/11/1999 1.000 .500 1.30   8/10/1999 .500 .531 .563
8/09/1999 .531 .531 .563   8/06/1999 .531 .563 .563
8/05/1999 .500 .500 .531   8/04/1999 .500 .594 .594
8/03/1999 .563 .594 .625   8/02/1999 .594 .656 .656
7/30/1999 .625 .656 .656   7/29/1999 .625 .688 .719
7/28/1999 .688 .750 .781   7/27/1999 .750 .688 .750
7/26/1999 .656 .656 .688   7/23/1999 .594 .563 .594
7/22/1999 .563 .531 .563   7/21/1999 .531 .563 .563
7/20/1999 .563 .625 .656   7/19/1999 .625 .719 .719
7/16/1999 .719 .750 .750   7/15/1999 .750 .875 .875
7/14/1999 .813 .750 .844   7/13/1999 .688 1.188 1.219
7/12/1999 1.188 .688 1.281   7/09/1999 .531 .438 .531
7/08/1999 .406 .375 12.000   7/07/1999 .344 .313 .406
7/06/1999 .313 .250 .313   7/02/1999 .281 .313 .313
7/01/1999 .281 .313 .313   6/30/1999 .281 .281 .281
6/29/1999 .281 .281 .313   6/28/1999 .281 .313 .313
6/25/1999 .313 .281 .344   6/24/1999 .313 .313 .344

If you look closely at the numbers in the chart above, you should have seen at least four separate occasions where FONX hit a support level around 28 to 30 cents. On those four occasions where the support level was reached, FONX popped back to 0.50-1.00 for a net gain of 100-300%. If the trend continued to hold true, any price below 28 cents would be a good buy-in point for this stock.

Technically, trend trading can be considered much the same as swing trading, as both methods of investing involve holding a stock for only a short period of time. The main difference between the two investment styles is that with swing trading you generally have some knowledge of an upcoming event, while trend trading is solely based on patterns.

One other thing I have noticed about trend trading is that often it doesn't matter what kind of shape the company is in. What do I mean? I have found that stocks stuck in a trend often stay in that trend. I once found a stock that bounced like a ping pong ball between 19 and 40 cents. Every time the stock hit 19 cents it quickly rebounded to 30 or 40 cents. I did a little DD on the company in question and I did not like what I saw. Everything about the company looked terrible. Little revenue, large debt, lawsuits, etc...This newfound information scared me off from investing in this particular company. Well, a few days later this stock hit 19 cents. I did not buy the stock per the aforementioned reasons, but I did keep my eye on it out of curiosity. Guess what happened? The stock opened at 19 cents the next day and closed at 32 cents just like the trends had predicted. I have seen this happen time and time again with companies that look like stinkers. Therefore, if I identify a trend I pounce on it no matter what the company situation is.

Daytrading

Unfortunately, daytrading is one investment style that does not work too well with penny stocks. Because many penny stocks have such large percentage based spreads, daytrading these securities is more difficult than doing the same with Dow or Nasdaq stocks. The stocks on the larger exchanges often have very tight spreads which makes daytrading them very easy. Daytrading a stock with a tight spread only requires a small movement in price to achieve a profit. So long as the bid rises above the asking price that you paid for the stock, you can make a profit by daytrading. The spread on a particular penny stock may only be three tenths of a cent (i.e. 0.040 x 0.043) but it could take a few days for the bid to rise above the asking price that you paid for the stock. In that case, this transaction becomes a swing trade rather than a daytrade. Of course, should a press release come out on the day you are attempting to daytrade the stock you should have no problem selling for a profit. However, under normal circumstances, the large spread makes daytrading penny stocks a difficult proposition.

IPO's

Everyone has seen the famous IPO scenario. A company IPO's (Initial Public Offering) at cheap prices and closes on its first day of trading with gains anywhere from 100-900%. Does the average investor get a shot at these gains? Absolutely not! When a stock IPO's, only certain investors of the brokerage firm that is underwriting the IPO are offered the opportunity to buy the stock at it's "official" IPO price. These investors are usually the biggest investors in the brokerage who have mountains of cash to play around with. These bigwigs get to buy the stock at say $15, but by the time the stock is offered to the general public it is selling for $80 a share. When the day's trading is done, the IPO stock may close at $75 for a "400% gain", but this is not really the case. Only those who were afforded the opportunity to buy the stock at the real IPO price get these gains. The average Joe like you and I did not have the chance to get in on these prices. Oh no. We had to pay $80 for these shares versus the $15 that the bigwigs got to pay. We lose and they win.

Well, I am happy to inform you that all of this is about to change. A new company has formed which will grant the average investor access to the IPO. The company itself delivers non-regulated services that center on education and building an online community of investors and investment clubs, entrepreneurs and service providers (attorneys, accountants, consultants, etc.). The company's subsidiary, IPOfactory, will deliver investment banking and other regulated services once it is licensed as a broker-dealer and investment adviser (no investment related services are available now). These two entities will work together to provide the average investor access to venture capital investing and an opportunity to grab a piece of the IPO action.

By creating a membership of thousands of individual investors, this company will have the power to offer aspiring businesses substantial venture capital. If 5,000 investors choose to invest $500 in an up and coming company, that translates into an infusion of 2.5 million dollars for the aspiring business. These 5,000 investors are given stock in the company that no one else can own. No one else can get stock in the company because it is privately traded and is not available on any of the exchanges. If the invested company plays its cards right and develops into a winner, it may go public and get listed on one of the national exchanges. Those 5,000 investors who backed the company in its infancy will come out the big winners.

So how can you join this company and grab a piece of the venture capital IPO action? Visit my website at http://www.pennystockbook.com/fs.htm for complete details.

When and How to Sell

One of the hardest things to do when investing is deciding when you want to sell your position in a security. There is no set method for determining your exit point. Only you can decide the price at which you will be comfortable selling. How much profit do you want to take home? Is 10% good enough for you, or do you want something a little higher? Remember, when we discussed planning earlier, I made a concerted effort to tell you that you must have an exit point established. Without a selling point you are setting yourself up for disaster.

When selling stock there are many different strategies that you can use. The first and simplest strategy is to sell your entire position when your stock has met your preset exit point. This method will take you out of a stock completely and is the least costly where commissions are concerned, because you only make one simple sale.

A second school of thought for selling stocks is the one half approach. This method of selling stock is very common among stock investors and has been around for quite some time now. The theory behind the one half approach is to sell half of your position in a stock once it has achieved a 100% gain. By doing so, you effectively remove your original investment from the market and continue trading with your remaining profits, which are equal to your original investment. I like this strategy because it protects your original investment and it allows you to retain a position in the stock should it continue to rise. Of course if the stock suddenly begins to tank, you can sell and still walk away with a nice profit.

A third method of selling stocks is to do so in increments. This way of selling stock is rarely used due to its high cost and labor intensiveness. With this method, you must set multiple exit points and sell a percentage of your holdings whenever these points are reached. The problem with this technique is that it involves multiple sales, effectively decreasing your profit margin once you account for the broker's commissions.

When it comes to selling stock, a common downfall of many investors is getting greedy. All too often, investors hold onto their stock longer than necessary as they try to squeeze just a little more profit out of their investment. Greed is an infectious process that can affect anyone including the savvy experienced investor. As I have mentioned many times in this book, it is best to sell your penny stock investment when a spike occurs. These spikes don't last long, so you must act quickly and decisively. If you allow greed to cloud your judgment, there is a great possibility that you will fail to take advantage of the spike. An example of this is evident with my friend Arthur. Arthur purchased a particular penny stock at a bargain price of 1.74 cents and he tucked it away into one of his many brokerage accounts. After holding the stock for a few months, it began to peak in the high 2 cent range on rumors of a pending business deal. This stock's historical high was in the low 3 cent range, so when it reached the upper deuce range I advised my pal to sell his position and take his profit. If he sold his shares when I advised him to do so, Arthur could have pocketed a nice profit of over 50%. Unfortunately, the greed virus had infected Arthur and he informed me that he felt the stock could rise much higher. With these thoughts in mind, Arthur held his stock. Over the next few weeks, news of the business deal never materialized and Arthur's stock fell back to 2 cents. Because of his greediness, my friend missed out on a nice profit. Learn from this lesson. Set a goal and sell when your stock achieves it. Do not allow greed to steal the profits from under your nose.

6

Shakeouts & Walkdowns

Disclaimer: *This chapter deals with the rumored actions of market makers. In no way or fashion is the information in this chapter meant to befoul the reputation of these trading professionals. This information is based solely on rumors and should therefore be treated as such.*

One of the most dreaded words in a penny stock trader's vocabulary is "shakeout". Shakeouts have cost many investors big bucks and will continue to do so as long as stocks are traded. Shakeouts occur when the bid/ask suddenly drops for no apparent reason. During a shakeout I have seen the bid/ask fall under the strangest of circumstances such as when the buys heavily outnumber the sells. Penny stocks are heavily controlled by the market makers and the shakeout is a prime example of this. The shake seems to affect the novice and those trading with "scared money" the most. As the price falls these folks often panic and sell for fear of losing their investment. I must admit that when I first started trading stocks I was a victim of a shakeout or two. Back then it seemed that right after I purchased a stock the price would suddenly fall. I would get scared and sell, taking a small loss, only to watch as the price rebounded to higher levels just a short time later. They say you learn best through personal experience and I believe it. After being burned by a few shakeouts, I began to seriously examine this market phenomenon.

First of all, why does a shakeout occur? It's simple really. The market makers need shares to sell to potential buyers. By performing a shakeout the market makers are able to buy up shares at a temporarily deflated prices. This allows them to accumulate shares and to cover their short positions. The market makers then turn around and sell those same shares at higher prices following the shake. This is easy money for them. Experienced investors know that it is best to hold and ride out the shakes. In fact, many seasoned investors use the shakeout as a buying opportunity, taking advantage of the short-lived dips in the price. If you monitor particular stocks, you will find that shakeouts tend to follow certain patterns, often happening at the same time of the day. Should you be shrewd enough to find these patterns, use them to your advantage and buy during the price dip. Shakeouts are one of the best times to purchase a stock.

While many may think of the shakeout as being a short-term phenomenon some shakes actually last for days or weeks. These long and drawn out shakes are more difficult to recognize than the quick shake. To accomplish the long shakeout market makers are rumored to use a tactic called "walking down" a stock. Here is how the walk down is supposed to work. Each day during the walk down the bid/ask slowly drop at a pace that doesn't cause great alarm. To offset investor fears, the bid/ask may actually gap up at the open and then resume the descent throughout the remainder of the day. Over the course of a week, the walk down can dissipate the value of a stock quite a bit. Rumor has it that the market makers continually load up on shares as the walk down occurs. When their positions are covered and enough shares are accumulated, the bid and ask may begin to rise again creating new demand for the stock. Now that interest in the stock has picked up again, the market makers can sell the shares acquired during the walk down for a lot more than what they paid for them. Of course, these are just rumors.

One of the unique things about penny stocks is the close camaraderie that exists between investors of the same stock. During a normal day of trading, penny stockholders often congregate on bulletin boards to discuss the day's action and to hunt for hot tips. When shakeouts do occur, the word usually gets out onto the bulletin board. More often than not, the true longs, long-term owners of the stock in question, will inform everyone of the impending shakeout. With experience, you will find that once you own a stock for a while, you can predict the shakeouts fairly accurately. If you are new to a stock and you suspect that a shakeout is occurring, ask one of the longs what is going on. The long will most likely recognize the shake and inform you to "hold and buy on the dips."

A true story here. A friend of mine had purchased a penny stock at 6.2 cents. This guy had done extensive DD on the company and had even gone so far as to speak with the company president on multiple occasions. My friend kept telling me that the stock was a bargain at six cents. It had recently hit a high of 16 cents not less than one month earlier and was experiencing the typical post-high slide. After purchasing the stock at 6.2 cents, my friend was feeling pretty good, because the stock immediately shot up to 6.8 cents. Over the next few weeks, things began to change. Trading volume on the stock began to drop significantly and press releases failed to materialize. The stock was not mentioned in any penny pick newsletters and it was hardly ever mentioned on the boards anymore. The stock tumbled, dropping a steady 4 to 5% everyday. There was an occasional pop in the price, but it was usually too small to offset the losses that the stock was experiencing. Bashers were having a field day with the stock as its price kept dropping. The stock hit five cents and my friend continued to hold. The stock hit four cents and my buddy still held his shares. When the stock began to drop below the four cent mark my pal started to worry, and he gave the president of the company another call. After speaking with him, my friend felt a little better about his investment. He continued to hold with hopes that the stock would soon turn around. He had done the DD on the company, he knew that the management was sound and the potential was there. These were the only reason he had held the stock throughout the slide. He must have really believed in that company because he had already lost almost 40% of his investment, yet he still refused to sell. As I spoke with him one evening, my pal confided in me that he was going to sell his position if the stock hit 3.5 or less. He had some upcoming expenses and he said that he could not risk losing any more money on his investment. As fate would have it, the stock continued to slide and my friend reluctantly sold his entire position at 3.6 cents, thus losing 42% on his original investment. My friend had become the victim of a walkdown. As the afternoon wore on he felt a little better about selling the stock because the bid had dropped to 3.4 cents and showed no sign of stopping. Unfortunately for my friend, about half an hour before the close there was a bombshell. A large DOW corporation that had a strategic alliance with my friend's former penny stock mentioned the company in a forward looking press release. In the final thirty minutes of trading his old penny stock shot through the roof. Large block buys came in from all directions and the bid/ask rose faster than a speeding bullet. At the end of the day the stock closed up over 22% for the day at a nickel. I got a phone call from my friend that night and he sounded ill. I asked him if he was feeling alright and then he told me what had happened. I felt very sorry for him. He had held the stock through its down days and staunchly supporting and defending it while others bashed it. Had he held just a few more hours, he could have ridden the stock as it climbed back to his original entry point. He said that he felt sick to his stomach thinking about what had happened. I told him not to worry about it. What's done is done and there is nothing he could do to change what had happened. Dwelling on things like that will eat you up inside. I told him to quit concentrating on his mistake and to think about how he could get back on his feet again. A pessimistic thinker would say, "I just lost 42% on my investment! Why does this always happen to me?" You must not think in this fashion, you must think positively to be successful. The optimistic thinker would say, "How can I regain that 42% I lost on my investment?" Do you see the difference in thought here? One person is dwelling on his mistakes while another is looking for ways to rectify them. I gave my friend a few leads on a couple of penny stock rumors I had been hearing and told him to check them out. My friend ended up putting all of his remaining funds into one particular stock, and lo and behold it shot up 80% in less than three days! My buddy had made back his entire investment and then some. Pretty amazing if you ask me, but anything is possible in the world of penny stocks.

> *You made how much?*
>
> -Common question that successful
> penny stock investors receive.

7

Subpenny Stocks

Holy cow! That subpenny stock you bought last week topped today's movers and shakers list with a 2000% gain. You're rich now, right? Well, I wouldn't run out and buy that new yacht just yet. Take a good look at the quote for your subpenny and tell me what you see. The bid/ask didn't change at all did they? Go ahead and say "bye-bye" to your so-called big gain because it never really existed. What is going on here? My friend, welcome to the wonderful world of the subpenny stock.

I was first attracted to the subpenny realm by false delusions of grandeur. I thought to myself if a four cent stock goes up one cent you have a 25% gain, but a one cent spike in a stock costing half a penny results in a 200% gain. Wow! Sounds pretty good, huh? With those thoughts in hand I began searching the internet for stocks costing less than one cent, but none were to be found. I had heard about these subpenny stocks on many of the bulletin boards that I frequented so I knew they existed. I continued looking and I finally hit paydirt when I checked the percent gainers list for the OTCBB market. What I found was simply amazing! Nearly every stock on the list had gains of close to 1000% for the day. Did you hear me? 1000% gains in a *single* day! Best of all, most of the stocks on the list began the day at subpenny prices. I was very excited having finally confirmed that these subpenny stocks did indeed exist and that they did achieve huge one-day gains. However, as I began to dig a little deeper my excitement turned to disappointment.

Let's take a closer look at the world of subpenny stocks. Right off the bat you should notice the substantial spread, the difference between the bidding and asking prices, on these stocks. The spreads are huge, up to two thousand percent in some cases. You read right, 2000%! It is not uncommon to see a subpenny bidding for 0.001 and asking 0.02. Who in their right mind is going to pay for a stock that must rise 2000% just to break even? Nobody! Just take a look at the daily average volume for these stocks; two hundred shares, four hundred shares, zero shares, etc...! Yes, many subpenny stocks may go for weeks or even months at a time with absolutely no trades at all. No trades mean no change in the bid/ask and no way for you to make that two thousand percent gain to break even from your buy-in point. Aside from the fact that many of these subpennies have outrageous spreads there are other substantial reasons why these stocks are a suspect investment. To begin with, nearly all subpenny companies do not file reports with the Securities and Exchange Commission. With the new OTCBB rules concerning SEC filing, many of these subpenny stocks are now on the pink sheets. Without SEC filings it is nearly impossible to get any trustworthy information on the company. What type of business is the company in? What do the company's financial statements look like? Is the company going bankrupt? Just try to answer these questions without the benefit of SEC 10K filings; you can't. Equally elusive as the SEC filings are company press reports. Can you find any press releases on any of the subpenny stocks? I've tried in vain to find some PR's from these businesses, and I can honestly say that it would be much easier to spot a UFO in the night sky. As a matter of fact, it is very difficult to find any information at all for these subpennies. No phone numbers. No business address. Nothing. Nada. The only information available for most of the subpenny stocks seems to spew from bulletin board posters. Where those guys found their information I haven't a clue. Perhaps they just make things up. It happens you know.

Would I invest my money in a subpenny stock? My answer is "No" but I might take a gamble on one. What do I mean by taking a gamble? Buying a subpenny stock is much like playing the lottery, however with a lotto ticket you can flip it over and see your odds of winning. With subpennies you are usually devoid of any information whatsoever. I would never place any substantial amount of money into a subpenny stock. With no solid company data these stocks just don't make sense as an investment. On occasions if I have a little extra cash burning a hole in my pocket I may pick up a few hundred bucks worth of a subpenny play. When dealing with subpennies I realize that I am gambling and not investing. To be honest, I actually anticipate losing the money I stick into the subpenny play. Now hold it just one minute! I'll bet that you are asking yourself this question, "If he plans on losing the money why did he even bother to buy that stock?" Remember that I said this was a gamble. On rare occasions subpenny stocks may suddenly jump up a few cents for no apparent reason. Those who are fortunate enough to be in the stock at the time can make a killing.

I know that on every board some guy swears that he bought into the stock back when it cost less than one cent. Is this guy lying? Maybe, maybe not. Personally, I think that most of these jokers look at the price history for the stock and discover that at one time it was indeed at subpenny levels. Maybe it makes them feel better to claim that they got into the stock at those levels. Who knows why they make those claims? The problem with looking at the price history for penny and subpenny stocks is that the list can be deceiving. The history may show a close at less than one cent, but that price was most likely the bid meaning that the stock closed for the day with the last trade being a sell. Note the few times that the stock closed over a penny; that price is most likely the ask. Simply compare the two prices, the bid versus the ask, and it looks as if the stock shot up big-time for the day. Now look at the volume history for the stock. Sometimes the stock may have one transaction for the day. A buy and the stock closes at the asking price "rising" hundreds of percentage points. A sell and the stock closes at the bidding price. Because the spread for these subpennies is so great it often appears as if these stocks make huge gains based on only one trade. Can you see why I don't believe those guys when they claim to have gotten into the stock at the subpenny prices?

If you really have a yearning to buy into a subpenny stock try to beat the spread by placing a limit order. If the stock you desire is priced 0.001 X 0.02 place a limit buy order for 0.005 just to see what happens. If the market makers decide to fill your order you will have cut one and one half cents off of the asking price. If the order doesn't fill simply try the same thing on another subpenny. Should you happen to actually ever purchase one of these stock please keep this in mind. The bid/ask on your stock may sit stagnant for months or even years. In some cases your subpenny stock may actually get delisted from the OTCBB market and your shares may as well be used for toilet paper! Hopefully, this will not happen. As stated in the "Golden Rules" earlier, be sure to constantly monitor the price of your subpenny stock. If there is ever a spike in the price, sell immediately and take your profits because there is no telling how long the drought between spikes will be. Although it has great profitability potential, the subpenny stock is a risky one and should be treated with extreme caution.

8

Other OTCBB Stocks

While they are not quite "penny stocks", OTCBB stocks costing one dollar or more can still provide great returns on your investment. In general, these stocks follow the same trading patterns and quirkiness of the penny stocks. They rise and fall at the drop of a hat and often fluctuate between 5 and 10% a day. Just because these stocks cost a little more, do not get fooled into thinking that these securities are like their Dow and Nasdaq counterparts. These stocks still belong to the OTCBB and they have the potential to rise and fall quickly, thus having great volatility.

Much like the penny stocks, OTCBB dollar stocks seem to move on rumors and momentum. Concepts of price to earnings ratios, earnings per share, etc...still seem to have little merit in the price movement of these stocks. It has been my experience that the best OTCBB dollar stocks to own are those that have rumors floating around the internet. A stock with rumors in its closet generates interest. This interest translates into heightened trading activity for the stock and greater price movement. Once the excitement over a stock has faded away, it is time to move on to another play. As I have said before, a stock with no interest generates no activity. This combination spells doom and gloom for a OTCBB stock. The following are a few examples of OTCBB dollar stocks I have recently profited from:

Example 1: BIDN

I originally heard about this stock from one of the hot tip boards on the internet. The phrase, "This stock is the next Ebay!" caught my eye and I decided to further investigate the lead. The company was called Bid Now.Com and they had the concept of promoting "live" auctions on the website. Then BIDN website had yet to open and this was the reason for the buzz on this stock. Many felt that BIDN could experience a nice run in anticipation of the website debut. I jumped into the stock with a humble position around nine dollars. As the website debut neared, excitement over BIDN reached a fever pitch and it was being mentioned on all of the reputable OTCBB newsletters and pick sites. Amidst all of this excitement, I have to chuckle when I remember posters saying that BIDN was going to be worth hundreds of dollars per share like EBAY was. Some guys even went so far as to say that BIDN was going to put EBAY out of business! With the excitement over BIDN, the price of its stock was destined to rise, and it did. Within a short period of time, BIDN stock rose from $9 to over $22. That is not too shabby for an OTCBB security. There are not too many stocks in this market that break the $20 barrier. Needless to say, those of us who jumped on BIDN early made nice profits during its run up to $22. However, all good things must come to an end and BIDN's run did just that.

After the unveiling of the BIDN website, interest in the stock began to fade. Many BIDN investors sold their positions to take profits and moved on to the next hot stock play. If I remember correctly, many of the BIDN investors I knew jumped onto another stock called IMOT. Not wanting to be left out of the crowd, I followed the group. As we went our separate ways from

BIDN, I would occasionally take a look at its quote just for grins. As I was writing this book, I was shocked to discover that this once mighty stock, which had at one time cost more than $22 per share, had declined to less than one dollar and was now trading on the pink sheets! That is quite a change! Fortunately, the other investors and I were lucky enough to take advantage of BIDN's excitement and walk away with big profits. It's like I said, you must monitor your OTCBB stocks closely and take profits whenever they materialize. If you fail to do so, you could end up getting burned by a situation similar to this one.

Example 2: IMOT

Following the sale of our BIDN stock, many of the investors in my group jumped onto a stock named IMOT. IMOT was in the business of providing internet services for China. I remember that some posters were calling IMOT the "Chinese Yahoo!" This sounded good to me and it must have sounded good to others as well because rumors began to surface about the stock. Once again I found myself involved with one of the hottest OTCBB stocks at the time. Like BIDN before it, IMOT was being mentioned in the OTCBB newsletters and pick sites. My friends and I had originally invested in IMOT around $5 and we eventually sold out when the stock passed $8. Not too bad. We made a nice profit from the stock; definitely a better return than anything we could have bought on the Dow! Our play on IMOT lasted for just a few days before we sold and moved on to the next hot ticket. Again, we took advantage of the rumors and sold on the spike. Currently, IMOT is nowhere near its former $8 glory. If you learn one thing from this book, please remember to take those profits on the spikes!

Example 3: XNET

Yes, this stock was mentioned earlier in the book. I have to admit, however, that I played XNET on more than one occasion. The last time I dealt with this stock, I was met with tremendous success in just a short period of time. I had originally heard about XNET from the same group of individuals whom I had traded BIDN and IMOT with. We first discovered XNET when it was a penny stock and we rode it up to a buck fifty. After selling and taking our profits, we moved on to other stocks. I like to keep my eye on stocks that treat me well, so I monitored XNET's activity for a few months.

After hitting $1.50, XNET stagnated and slowly declined to around $1. At this point, I was very involved with a number of other stocks so I quit looking at the XNET quote for a while. The next time I examined the XNET quote I was stunned to see that it had climbed its way over $2. Sensing the beginning of another run on XNET stock, I took a position in the security on the following day in the upper $2 range. Fortunately, XNET had a great surge within the next few days reaching its all time high over $6. Once again, I sold on the spike and took my profits while they were hot. XNET sold off and then returned to the $1 to $2 dollar range for a while. Well, recent developments with China and the World Trade Organization made XNET a hot commodity. XNET, I am happy to say, has had the good fortune of rising as high as $20 a share following these developments. Unfortunately, I sold my XNET a long time ago. Ugghhh! To think that I once owned a ton of this stock when it was less than a buck! Oh well, life goes on.

As you can see, OTCBB dollar stocks have the potential to be just as profitable as the OTCBB penny stocks. Do not limit yourself to just one or the other. If you see a hot dollar stock play, do not hesitate to jump on it. Hesitation can cost you money and is counterproductive to your investment objectives. The successful investor recognizes as many opportunities as possible. Whether it manifests in a penny or dollar stock, take advantage of all that the OTCBB market has to offer. Remember, sell on the spikes and take your profits while they exist! No one ever went broke by taking a profit. However, I do know guys who have lost incredible sums of money because they didn't sell on the spikes. Greed got the best of these people; they held their positions just a little too long with hopes that the spike would last forever. Well, the spikes don't last long and these guys are now stuck with cheap stock that could have made them big profits had they sold when the chance was there. Remember Arthur?

> *No one ever went broke by taking a profit.*
>
> - Anonymous post from a penny stock
> message board.

9

The Bulletin Board Community

Bulletin boards are great. Without these vital gathering places such as Raging Bull and Bobz.com, information about penny stocks would be very hard to come by. Bulletin boards are commonly referred to simply as "the boards". Investors flock to these internet sites to find the latest gossip and rumors about their favorite stock or just to chat with old friends. A myriad of colorful characters can always be found on the boards. Hypsters, bashers, newbies, longs, and shorts all post their two cents worth. The art of dissecting a bulletin board can be very tricky. Who can you trust? How can you distinguish rumors from facts? Should you respond to that guy who just called you an idiot for your last post? I like to compare the boards to the wild west of yesteryear. Each board seems to have its good guys and its villains. One thing is for sure, there is very little regulation as to what can be posted on the boards. If you think about it, it would be nearly impossible for a bulletin board service to monitor all of its posts. Raging Bull has over 5,000 boards alone and some of them have up to 65,000 posts on them. Many of the board services will post a disclaimer releasing them from liability where the posts are concerned. The board services even go so far as to warn the newcomer that all information posted on the boards cannot be trusted. Most board services will have someone you can contact via email to report violations and the SEC has a site where you can report those who post false or illegal information. Other than that there is very little regulation about what can be posted on a board.

Longs

Once you spend enough time on the boards, you discover who is trustworthy and who is not. In most cases the "longs," guys who have held a stock for an extended period of time, seem to be your safest bet for a trusty poster. The longs usually do not hype their stock because they are comfortable with their investment. This is probably because most longs have done sufficient DD and feel confident with the stock. Because they have usually done such extensive DD, longs are often good sources of information. Once you have identified a "long" on your board utilize him or her to gather information and to answer questions you may have about the stock. For example, ask the long about the trading patterns for the stock. Does the stock tend to gap up after days with big gains? What time during the day do the market makers usually perform a shakeout? Some penny stocks follow very set patterns and the longs will recognize this. Gap up at the open, dip about two hours later, a lull during lunch, and a run up before the bell may be a typical pattern for a certain penny stock. I have noticed that once I have held a penny stock for a long time, I can almost predict exactly what is going to happen on certain days since the market makers for particular stocks tend to fall into daily routines. Of course, I am not always right. But on occasions, I have accurately predicted what a stock will do and I have used that knowledge to maximize my profits. Most longs will know the history of the stock they hold. Remember to trust the longs and don't be afraid to ask them questions. I can guarantee that they will be more than happy to answer your queries.

Newbies

At the opposite end of the spectrum exists the "newbie." Newbies are the people who have just recently purchased a stock and they usually don't have any clue about it. Some newbies don't even know what the company in which they have just purchased stock in does for business! The longs and newbies are easy to spot on the boards and are often very nice folks to talk to. Newbies often ask the questions and longs are usually the ones who will answer. I have found, however, that the newbie is the investor most likely to hype a stock. Newbies want their stock to do well and they may post a lot of hype on the boards in order to pump their stock. Newbies are also the investors most likely to sell during a shakeout. As the newbie learns from experience in the school of hard knocks, he or she will eventually become a seasoned, savvy investor.

Hypsters

Let us now take a look at the guys who really make the bulletin boards tick: the "hypster" and the "basher." These two characters are the ones who give a board its personality. The hypster is easily recognizable because he sticks out like a sore thumb. This guy usually has more posts than a barbed wire fence on a Texas ranch. His posts are numerous, repetitive and full of wild claims and bogus information. Claims such as, "this stock will hit $1 soon" and, "big block buys are coming " are typical of the hypster. My personal favorites are often used by the newbies and they generally sound like, "this stock rules" and, "this baby rocks!" Who cares? The hypster is full of hot air and baloney. He never gives any solid information to verify his claims and he will usually act in an immature manner when anyone disputes his posts.

A classic example of a hypster is Mr. X. On one particular Sunday, I noticed Mr. X spamming the boards with stock AREE. For those of you unaware of spamming, it is an act of mass solicitation. In one single day, Mr. X made 150 posts to over 60 boards and did some additional spamming under other assumed aliases. Often when a hypster goes to this extreme his strategy will begin to backfire. People get so sick and tired of seeing his posts that they tune him out. Hypsters are red flags for pump and dump stocks. When you see a lot of hypsters pumping a certain stock be cautious. Hypsters are usually involved in the pump and dumps or they are guys who bought into a stock at its high and are trying to regenerate interest in their investment. I saw an example of this with stock HIJK.

HIJK had just hit a new high on unusually heavy trading volume and a lot of newbies jumped on the bandwagon. On the following day HIJK tanked 40% in a huge profit taking sell off. These new investors were stuck with an eight cent stock which they had just paid 14 cents for on the previous day. The newbies must have been scared because that same night I saw them out spamming the boards with some bogus rumor about a possible company buyout. There was no truth to this buyout rumor and everyone knew it. These guys were simply hyping the stock in order to generate an artificial run. The next day HIJK fell an additional ten percent and the rumors about the buyout ceased. What is my point you ask? My point is that you can never trust a hypster. Always verify the hypster's claims. If his claims cannot be verified as true the hypster is most likely feeding you bogus information and it would be in your best interest to ignore him.

Bashers

While the hypster tries his hardest to make you buy a particular stock, the "basher" does his best to make you sell your hard-earned investment. How many times have you gone to your favorite board only to see some jerk making crazy posts such as, "SELL THIS DOG NOW!" or, "THIS STOCK WILL TANK TOMORROW!"? I see it all of the time, and the bashers never cease to amaze me with their wild and crazy posts. Many may wonder why a person would try to drive the price of a stock down. It's simple really; there are a few possible scenarios that motivate bashers. Scenario number one: the basher once owned the stock in question, sold it for a profit, and now he wants the price to dip so he can get back in again at a lower price. Scenario number two: the basher has lost money on the stock in question and is getting "revenge" by trying to tank the price. Some people just get their kicks by angering other investors; believe me, I've seen it happen. A guy who gets burned by a stock is more than happy to go and bad mouth it to all. Compared to the hypsters, the basher has a much simpler task at hand. It is much easier to scare someone into selling a stock than it is to convince someone to buy one.

The basher will take any information he can find on a stock and twist it into a frightening message. For example, anytime a penny stock has a dip in price, the basher will claim that the stock is tanking. The basher conveniently forgets to mention that the same penny stock just had a 50% gain yesterday and that the current dip in the price is only 10% of the previous day's gain. Bashers, the good ones, often have very intimate knowledge of the stocks that they trash. These unscrupulous fellows will often take information out the company's 10K and 10QSB reports and use it to their advantage. The SEC 10K filing lists company financial data in addition to other information such as current pending lawsuits. As is the case with most beginning ventures the financial data for many penny stock companies is not what one would call stellar. These businesses tend to have large start up debt and minimal revenues. The bashers will use the financial data in the 10K to scare investors into selling. If the financials were so bad, why wouldn't you sell? Well, the answer is simple. When investing in penny stock companies you are taking a big risk. The risk you take is entrusting your hard-earned money to a company you hope will become profitable as their business develops. With penny stocks, as with large cap stocks, you are investing in the *future* value of the company. The key words here are future value. Bashers don't look to the future; they dwell on the past. Concerning lawsuits, remember that almost all businesses have lawsuits pending against them. The basher will use the pending legal proceedings from the 10K as ammunition for their trade. Lawsuits sound scary and the basher knows this. It is a simple fact that legal proceedings are a way of life for today's business community. The basher doesn't tell you this, however, he only focuses on how the pending lawsuits will "bring the company down".

A good basher can take totally legitimate information and use it to scare off the novice investor. Newbies, unfortunately, are the usual victims of the bashing community. A common practice in today's business world is using company shares as leverage in making purchases and acquisitions. An example of this is when Yahoo purchased Geocities for a combination of cash and company shares. The basher can take this totally benign information and use it scare off a newbie by claiming that the purchasing company is short on cash and is resorting to using their shares as a means to pay the bills. How can these guys get away with such dastardly tactics? Doesn't the SEC monitor guys like this? The sad truth is that these bashers are very smart folks. They know that the SEC is watching them like the proverbial big brother. So what does the basher do to avoid the long arm of the law? Words such as "possibly, could, may, and might" protect the basher from the law. These few little words change a basher's statements from fact to fiction. A smart basher would never say, "This company is a scam!" The smart basher, the one who stays out of prison, says "Caution! This company *may* be a scam!" Do you see the difference?

Sometimes when a basher is in true form and the price of the stock in question happens to be dropping for the day, the attention on the message board will often stray from the stock and shift towards the basher. I have seen it time and time again...message boards that focus on the basher rather than the stock. As the basher infuriates the other posters with his negative comments many investors will respond to him with threatening and derogatory comments. This is just what the basher wants, to create confusion and turmoil on the message board. Newcomers to the board may see all of this infighting and get scared into selling their shares, thus fulfilling the basher's goal. I remember one guy in particular, let's call him RJ. I was involved in a particular penny stock that was experiencing a nice run and ol' RJ jumped in at about seven and a half cents. RJ was a regular on the board for the next few days proclaiming himself to be long on the stock until it hit a dollar. Boy was he wrong! A few days down the road the stock underwent a major shakeout. I'm talking about a major shakeout here! The price of our stock had dropped over 40% in just a few days and the bashers were having a field day. "Sell, sell!" they exclaimed, "This dog has run its course!" RJ, the scared little newbie that he was, took the bashers comments to heart and sold his shares at a nickel. Following his sale RJ, the self-proclaimed long, began to bash the stock with great abandon. RJ did not bash for monetary reasons or personal gain. RJ was simply very upset that he had lost money and he wanted to vent his frustrations on the rest of the remaining shareholders. I felt sorry for RJ. I knew that we had a winner and I tried to tell RJ to hold and ride out the shake. Unfortunately, RJ fell for the basher's baloney. A few days after the shakeout our stock hit an all-time high of fourteen cents. I giggled a bit as I wondered how hard RJ was kicking himself.

While most seem to think that bashers are bad for a stock, I would like to offer a reason why bashers are actually a good sign for a stock. Bashers are an intelligent lot. These guys play the game for profits pure and simple. Think about it, if a stock was truly a dog as some of the bashers claim why would they hang around the board? If a penny stock was truly dead in the water the bashers would avoid it like the plague. A dead stock makes no movement. No movement equals no profits to be made. No profits to be made equals no bashers. Do you see where I am going with this? The mere presence of bashers on a board indicates that a stock is still a hot commodity. When the bashers disappear and the trading volume begins to dry up it is time to worry. No bashers and a drop in volume indicate that a penny stock has lost the attention of the market. This spells doom for a penny stock. So, as I have pointed out, bashers are not always bad for a stock. True, they may get under your skin, but bashers are a necessary evil for a stock to be successful. How should you deal with these deviant characters? Just ignore them. Bashers are very easy to spot. Of course, the content of their posts gives them away, but in addition, many basher's like to type in ALL CAPS in order to garner attention. ALL CAPS posts are bashers 9 times out of 10. Remember, the basher doesn't care about you and he is no good Samaritan. Bashers only care about themselves and their profits. Ignore them and save yourself a headache.

Unfortunately many bashers revert to shameless name-calling and the use of profanity in their posts. These bashers should not be confused with the professionals. Professional bashers generally stick to the stock they are tormenting and do not post personal messages. Should you happen to come across a basher that is using profanity and/or racial slurs report the poster to the webmaster of the message board. The webmaster will recognize that the basher is violating the terms of service agreement and should remove the culprit immediately.

The Master

I have spent a lot of time on the bulletin boards for penny stocks and I have seen my fair share of hypsters and bashers. I have seen the best and the worst that posters have to offer. Most hypsters and bashers are immature and post information that is of little consequence to the typical investor. There is one poster, however, whom I have watched weave magic better than anyone I have ever seen. This particular poster is known by many different aliases and no one knows if this person is a man or a woman. As a matter of fact, no one knows if this person is part of a group or if he/she works alone. For the sake of this story I will refer to the poster as a man and will call him Wall Street.

Wall Street must be a master psychologist/strategist because he always keeps the board guessing. No one seems to know anything about this guy. Some of his aliases have feminine names while others are masculine. The tone of his posts has a woman's touch, but the ruthlessness of his actions leads you to believe that he is man. Sometimes Wall Street refers to himself as an individual investor while other times he claims to be part of a large penny stock conglomerate. Whatever the case, Wall Street can be found working his mojo on many boards as he always seems to be involved in multiple penny stocks. Wall Street's plan is so simple that it is amazing that others do not copy him. Wall Street buys large blocks of stock while they are cheap and he hypes them like a madman. Because he buys these stocks at such low prices, they almost always go up as Wall Street lures in new investors with his incredible pumping. As the stock increases in price, Wall Street slowly dumps his shares into the market via multiple small sales so he doesn't draw attention. After dumping his shares for a hefty profit, Wall Street begins to bash the stock in an effort to drive the price down again. Wall Street is not your average basher. He only uses facts in his bashing and that is what really frightens investors. Bashing with facts keeps Wall Street out of trouble with the SEC. To further cover his backside, Wall Street uses terms such as "possibly" and "potential" in his more speculative postings. Most bashers use tactics such as name-calling and speculation, but not our master pump and dumper. Wall Street is one smart cookie. He reads the company's SEC 10K filings and recent press releases. As I explained earlier, most companies in the penny stocks market are young ventures and lack the cash or revenue that the larger DOW and Nasdaq companies have. Wall Street will use items in the 10K such as a company's poor financial standing and lack of revenue generation to scare off newbies. Wall Street knows how to play on people's emotions. When a stock is tanking he will be sure to let you know it and he likes to give predictions as to how far the stock will slide. Wall Street can become very irritating at times because he sometimes posts up to 50 messages per day. These messages often repeat themselves and they serve only one purpose, getting investors to sell their shares and drive the price of the stock down. Once the stock has dropped to Wall Street's predetermined rally point, he will once again begin to buy up large chunks of the stock. Wall Street now changes his alias and the cycle repeats itself. I have seen Wall Street do this for many months and I am sure that he has made a killing using these methods. Some may call these ways unethical or unscrupulous, but one thing is for sure, Wall Street is a rich man because of them.

Over the next few pages I have listed some examples of how Wall Street works his voodoo on a stock. In order to protect both the poster and the stock, I have changed the names for this story. For your complete understanding of this tale, allow me to give some background information on the stock in question. ABCD was a young company that opened for business in 1995. Like most new ventures, ABCD had a large debt and lack of revenue. The company had to resort to printing additional shares of stock to pay for services such as lawyer's fees and financial auditing. ABCD was named as a defendant in multiple lawsuits and had a recent rash of insider selling. This company sounds horrible doesn't it? Now let's take a look at what the company had going for it on the plus side. First and foremost, the company filled a niche in a potentially explosive industry. Second, ABCD had recently signed alliances with some major NYSE companies. Third, and this is definitely the most important, ABCD was rumored to have a website opening within a month. You must remember that penny stocks do not follow the traditional views of NYSE and Nasdaq stocks. Financial woes, lawsuits, P/E ratios, etc…all have very little meaning in the world of penny stocks. News releases, rumors, momentum…these are the things that fuel the penny stock realm. At the beginning of this story, ABCD sat at 2.6 cents. As events began to unfold, ABCD made an incredible climb to 15 cents and then tanked in a sell-off. Now you have the background for the story. Because Wall Street often makes over 40 to 50 posts per day, I have selectively chosen only a few of his postings for this story. Let's see what he has to say:

Post 1: Wall Street ~ "Wall Street group is in with 2.9 million shares"

We have 2.9 million shares at an average price of 2.1 cents. We see this stock hitting 10 cents by the end of the month. Our last pick achieved a 1000% gain in less than a month. We see the same potential here.

Post 2: Wall Street ~ "Level 2 shows big block buys coming!"

Man we are good. MM's moving up the bid/ask on level 2. Big block buys going to create a nice afternoon rally. Get in now before the run-up!

Post 8: Wall Street ~ "WOW! ABCD up 10% on heavy volume! Look for a nice gapper in the morning"

Great day for ABCD with close at 2.9 cents! Look for an opening tomorrow of 3 cents or higher. We see ABCD at 10 cents by end of the month.

Post 16: Wall Street ~ "AMAZING! ABCD ask up to 3.8 in first hour of trading!"

14 million shares traded in first hour today! Bid/ask moving up fast! Get in now while you can. Look for a close today at 5 cents.

Post 28: Wall Street ~ "ABCD 10K filing looks great! We have upped our target price on this stock to 14 cents!"

All investors should read the 10k filing for ABCD. This company shows real promise and is taking all of the right steps to become a major player in the industry. We now see ABCD at 14 cents by month's end and $1 by year's end.

Post 35: Wall Street ~ "Multiple PR's expected soon! ABCD will fly on the news!"

We have just confirmed that ABCD is preparing to unleash some stellar press releases that will create a buying frenzy!

Post 44: Wall Street ~ "NEWS OUT ON WEBSITE OPENING! TOLD YA SO!"

New website will place ABCD into e-commerce bonanza. We told you PR was coming! Hope you listened to us. Are we good or what? We now see ABCD at 30 cents by month's end. Get in while you can rookies!

Post 48: Wall Street ~ "ABCD now a dot.com business. This is a no brainer!"

Only a fool would pass up a golden opportunity like this! All dot.com businesses are money making machines! We're in with 4.5 million shares. This is a sure thing! Man we are good!

Post 53: Wall Street ~ "Ask up to .09 and climbing. Website opens in 5 days! We see ABCD at .30 by launch date"

Look for a huge run on ABCD between now and when the website opens! We plan on adding at least 2 million additional shares to our holdings between now and the opening of the website. Smart investors will listen to us.

Post 68: Wall Street ~ "WOW! 1 million share block trade @ the ask! Level 2 shows more huge buys coming and bid/ask rising!"

Here comes the run sports fans! We told you to get in when ABCD was under a dime. Still a good buy at 11 cents. We see ABCD at 30 cents when website opens. Better buy now while you can still afford to!

Post 83: Wall Street ~ "2 days until website opens. Buy now before the run-up!"

Only 48 hours left until website opening! We are expecting huge gains as daytraders flock to this stock over the next few days. We plan on selling at 40 cents. Our new Ferraris are already ordered!

Post 99: Wall Street ~ "WOW! 8 Million shares traded in first 30 minutes today! Ask up to 13 cents and rising! YEEHAAAWWW!"

Here we go! Level 2 shows nothing but buys coming in. Bid/ask rising fast! We told you this was going to happen! Man we are good! YEEHAAAWWWW!

Now the tide turns. Stock ABCD topped out at 15 cents and is being sold off by profit takers. Wall Street sells his shares, changes his handle to "Stock_Man and begins his tortuous bashing of the stock.

Post 108: Stock_Man ~ "ABCD TANKING AS INVESTORS ARE DISAPPOINTED WITH WEBSITE"

THE ABCD WEBSITE IS A JOKE! MY KID CAN DESIGN A BETTER WEBSITE THAN THAT! GLAD I SOLD AT 14 CENTS.

Post 118: Stock_Man ~ "ITS AN ABCD BLOOD BATH! SELL NOW AND CUT YOUR LOSSES. SUB-DIME LEVELS SOON."

WE TOLD YOU TO SELL AT 14 CENTS. ABCD IS DROPPING LIKE A ROCK. LONGS GETTING BURNED. WE SEE ABCD UNDER A DIME BY TODAY'S CLOSE.

Post 126: Stock_Man ~ "LEVEL 2 SHOWS BLOCK SELLS COMING! ABCD AFTERNOON RALLY FIZZLES."

ABCD RALLY IS OVER. BIG SELLS COMING. NO ONE WANTS TO HOLD THIS STOCK OVER THE WEEKEND. GET OUT NOW BEFORE YOU LOSE EVERYTHING!"

**Post 140: Stock_Man ~ "400 MILLION SHARES =
                              POSSIBLE REVESRE SPLIT"**

WITH THIS MANY SHARES IN THE FLOAT A
REVESRE SPLIT IS VERY LIKELY. A REVERSE
SPLIT WILL BURN ALL ABCD STOCKHOLDERS.
THINGS LOOK BAD FOR SHAREHOLDERS. NOT
TOO LATE TO GET OUT.

**Post 141: Stock_Man ~ "ABCD LOST 4 MILLION DOLLARS
                              LAST YEAR AND HAD ONLY
                              $35,000 IN REVENUE."**

THESE FINANCIALS ARE SCARY. READ THE 10K
FILING ROOKIES AND SEE WHAT A MISTAKE YOU
HAVE MADE. NOT A GOOD TIME TO BE AN ABCD
INVESTOR.

**Post 142: Stock_Man ~ "ABCD NAMED IN MULTIPLE
                              LAWSUITS"**

ABCD STANDS TO LOSE MILLIONS AS MULTIPLE
LAWSUITS ARE PENDING AGAINST THE
COMPANY. IT'S ALL IN THE 10K.

**Post 144: Stock_Man ~ "BID AT .056 AND FALLING. WE
                              SEE ABCD AT 4 CENTS BY NEXT
                              WEEK." (eom)**

**Post 146: Stock Man ~ " SEC MAY HALT TRADING OF
ABCD SOON."**

IT IS OBVIOUS THAT SOMETHING FISHY IS GOING
ON WITH THIS STOCK. SEC MAY HALT TRADING
AND INVESTIGATE. PENDING DISASTER.

**Post 149: Stock Man ~ " WOW! LOOK AT ALL OF THE
144'S FILED LATELEY. INSIDERS
ARE SELLING THIS DOG BEFORE
IT DROWNS!"**

LOOK AT ALL OF THE FORM 144'S FILED LATELY!
THE INSIDERS ARE DUMPING THEIR SHARES. DO
THEY KNOW SOMETHING THAT YOU DON'T?
BETTER SELL NOW WHILE YOU CAN!

**Post 150: Stock_Man ~ "ABCD AT SUBPENNY LEVELS
SOON! LONGS GETTING
BURNED!"**

I FEEL SORRY FOR THOSE WHO GOT SUCKERED
IN AT 14 CENTS. THE LONGS CONTINUE TO
SUCKER INVESTORS WITH THEIR SLIMEBALL
HYPE AND LIES. THIS STOCK IS GOING
SUBPENNY SOON!

I think you've seen enough. Do you see how this guy toys
with the rookie investors? Wall Street has gone through this cycle
many times and he does so on multiple stocks. Most people
recognize Wall Street's messages no matter what alias he posts
under, but he perseveres with his plan nonetheless. I cannot begin

to fathom how much money this guy has made playing penny stocks. He has obviously done well, otherwise he would not spend so much time and effort bashing and pumping these penny stocks. Guys like Wall Street are the ones who give penny stocks their "questionable" reputation. Because penny stocks are not yet as widely traded as their NYSE and Nasdaq counterparts, guys like Wall Street continue to have the ability to manipulate penny stocks. Many penny stock investors are indeed rookie investors trying their hand at the world of securities trading for the very first time and many conscienceless scoundrels are just dying to take advantage of them. Be on the look out for Wall Street and others like him. If you should happen to run across this person or anyone like him do yourself a favor and ignore them.

The Board and You

When you decide to invest in penny stocks you will inevitably be drawn to the bulletin board community. The boards provide a forum for you to communicate with other penny stock investors and are some of the best places to hear the latest rumors floating around the internet. There are a plethora of boards to post on, but two sites dominate the world of penny investing. Ragingbull.com is an outstanding site consisting of hundreds of message boards for nearly every penny stock imaginable. In addition, this website also has boards specifically devoted to hot stock tips, hidden gems, and subpenny stocks. Ragingbull offers a unique feature that allows you to "ignore" certain posters. Tired of reading the repetitive posts from a basher trashing your stock? Put him on "ignore". What a great feature! A second penny stock website well worth looking at is Bobz.com. Bobz is a site that is entirely devoted to hot stock tips. Penny stock investors command this board and it is not uncommon for this site to see thousands of different posts everyday. One unique feature offered by Bobz is the labeling of each post with the poster's personal ISP number. No matter how many aliases someone posts under, the same ISP number appears next to the post. This feature helps in identifying hypsters and bashers who are trying to manipulate a stock.

So you have purchased a penny stock and now you want to talk to your fellow investors. You will first need to pick a website that offers message boards or chat rooms. Once you have decided on a site that you feel comfortable with you will need to come up with a "handle", the name that you will post under. When devising your handle you will need to be very creative because other posters have already taken most of the typical names. Your handle should be well thought out because this name is what people are going to associate with your message. If your name sounds negative people may assume that you are a basher. Be creative!

Now that you have decided upon a website and a handle to post messages under, you must decide what type of poster you will be. There are many different personality types on the boards. Some posters are reserved, electing to remain in the shadows reading messages but rarely posting any of their own. Other posters have the exact opposite mentality as they make concerted efforts to try to run the board. After spending some time on the boards, you will notice that there is usually one or two guys who try to dominate the board. These folks tend to make numerous postings and will usually try to answer all questions that appear on the board. Of course, there are the normal posters who use the board as it was intended as they converse in a friendly and appropriate manner. Some of the posters who frequent the same board will become good friends with one another. Often, when their stock is not moving much, these posters will usually discuss off topic events such as last night's baseball game or the latest news. It can be a rewarding experience when you make a few good pals on the boards. Unfortunately, in addition to these posters you will always find your typical bashers, hypsters, pumpers and dumpers. So how will you post? Most new posters tend to be a little reserved and do not put forth many messages. They will often ask questions and prod the other posters for their feelings about the stock. It is usually best for new posters to just be themselves when typing messages.

If you are going to use the boards as a simple place for conversation, there is no reason for you to alter your normal personality. On the other hand, should you decide that you want to bash or hype a stock, there are a few things that you should keep in mind. If you are going to try your hand at hyping a stock, be sure to focus on the future potential of the company. Do not create false rumors such as a "potential buyout" or "possible merger". These tactics are a red flag for bogus hype. Penny stock companies are rarely purchased or acquired by other businesses. If you post junk like that people will identify you as a classic hypster and will ignore your postings. Use the forward looking statements from press releases as ammo for your hype. This information seems more credible as other investors can easily verify it. By all means, please avoid saying things like "XYZ RULES!" I hope I don't need to tell you why. Hyping works best when multiple posters work together. One person hyping a stock is commonplace, but many people hyping a stock tends to draw attention. When a stock has a good day the hypsters tend to come out in full force predicting everything under the sun. Sometimes too much hype can turn others off. Therefore, don't overdo it when hyping. Get your point across quickly and efficiently. If you post on a general stock tip board such as Bobz, I have found a little trick that I would like to share with you.

When posting on the general hot tip sites, avoid mentioning the name of your stock in the title of your message. From experience, I have noticed that more people read posts that do not mention a stock in the title. For example, if you were going to hype BICO, make your title read, "***THIS WEEK'S HOTTEST STOCK!!!!*****". I guarantee that this title will get many more hits than one such as, "***BICO IS A GREAT BUY!!!***". More people will click on the first message because their curiosity is aroused. Once they have opened your message, the curious poster will read it just to see what it says. The second message has no allure. If someone has no interest in BICO, they are not going to open the message and your effort is wasted. Keep this little gem in mind for future posts.

Bashing. Many investors have this style of posting down to an art. It is very easy to separate the good bashers from the rookies. First of all, why would you want to bash a stock? Bashing a stock can be a strategic weapon in your arsenal of tricks. If you like a particular stock, but it is priced just a bit too high for your taste, you may try bashing the stock to drive the price down. Personally, I abhor bashers, but there is real logic behind their methods. If you do bash a stock, be sure to stick to the facts. Factual information scares investors much more than speculation. Read the SEC 10K filings and note the lawsuits and company financial standing. More often than not, these two items will provide plenty of firepower for your bashing plans. For your own safety, DO NOT post false information about a stock. This is how you can get into legal trouble. Stick to the facts and you should remain safe.

Here is an example of what can happen to you when you do not follow these rules. Not long ago, two young men made an attempt to manipulate a stock by using false rumors to inflate its price. The two men in question purchased large quantities of NEI Webworld, Inc. and then using dozens of different aliases, they circulated rumors of a takeover. At sites such as RagingBull, Free Real Time, and Yahoo Finance, these men made claims that NEI was a takeover target of a telecommunications company called LCG Wireless. As rumor of this takeover spread, NEI stock prices soared from 13 cents up to 15 dollars per share! The two cyberbandits then allegedly sold their holdings and walked away with a cool $350,000 in profit. Following this run, NEI tanked and fell back to .25 per share, thus leaving many investors very unhappy. Well, you'll be happy to know that the law finally caught up to these guys. In early January 2000, a federal grand jury indicted the two men on conspiracy to commit securities fraud and wire fraud. If convicted on all counts, these men may face up to 15 years in prison and a 2.25 million dollar fine!

Appendix A:

Penny Stock Internet Links

General Search Engines:

1. http://www.yahoo.com

2. http://www.excite.com

3. http://www.lycos.com

4. http://www.altavistafinance.com

5. http://home.snap.com

6. http://www.go2net.com

7. http://www.hotbot.com

8. http://www.ionsearch.com

9. AOL has general search engine

Penny Stock Newsletters

1. http://www.smallstocks.com/

2. http://www.angelfire.com/ca3/stockpicks/

3. http://thepowerpick.listbot.com/

4. http://www.cyberstocks2000.com/join.htm

5. http://www.hotyellow98.com/lasercart/

6. http://www.explosivepick.com

7. htsk@iname.com

8. Stk2Watch@aol.com

9. http://www.angelfire.com/biz3/rags2riches

10. http://pennystockgazette.listbot.com

11. http://www.microcapworld.com

12. http://bullrunpick.listbot.com

13. http://home.att.net/~the-alliance-group/index.html

14. http://www.TheStockBoys.com

15. http://www.NOHYPENOBULL.com

Penny Stock Message Board and Chat Sites:

1. http://www.ragingbull.com

2. http://www.bobz.com

3. http://www.clearstation.com

4. http://www.techstocks.com

5. http://www.pennypicks.com

6. http://www.stockclub.com

7. http://www.stock-talk.com

8. http://www.smallstocks.com

9. http://chat.yahoo.com/?room=investments@news

10. http://www.iionline.com/boards

11. http://www.kingfine.com/cgi-bin/board.cgi?penny+0+++

12. http://www.chat.lycos.com

13. http://www.profitpicks.com/chat.htm

14. http://www.excite.com

15. http://www.fools-gold.com

Penny Stock Message Boards and Chat Sites Continued...

16.   http://www.clubs.yahoo.com/clubs/wallstreetu

17.   http://www.clubs.yahoo.com/clubs/zoomingstocks

18.   http://www.clubs.yahoo.com/clubs/stocksurfers

19.   http://www.clubs.yahoo.com/clubs/momostocks

20.   http://www.clubs.yahoo.com/clubs/hotstocks1

21.   http://www.clubs.yahoo.com/clubs/aaahotstocks

22.   http://www.stockhouse.com/bullboards

23.   http://www.quicken.com/investments/discuss

24.   http://pennies.net

25.   http://onlinestocks.org

26.   http://www.ddinvestor.com

27.   AOL has numerous chat rooms for discussing penny stocks

Penny Stock Picks and Rumor Sites

1. http://www.profitpicks.com/rumors

2. http://www.daytraders.com

3. http://www.angelfire.com/in2/pennystockpicks

4. http://www.pennypicks.com

5. http://www.freeyellow.com/members7/onza/penneypicks.html

6. http://www.xpenny.com/

7. http://www.freenet.tlh.fl.us/~duaneion/stock.htm

8. http://members.aol.com/stk2watch/hotpick.html

9. http://www.pennyinvestor.com/

10. http://www.wcon-line.com

11. http://www.geocities.com/WallStreet/District/7516/

12. http://www.fools-gold.com

13. http://sotm.com

14. http://pennystocks.bizhosting.com/

15. http://www.stockwinners.com

Penny Stock Picks and Rumor Sites Continued

16. http://www.talweb.com/duane/Hot/index.htm

17. http://members.aol.com/jskowboy/index.html

18. http://www.freeyellow.com:8080/members7/stockjungle

19. http://www.freeyellow.com:8080/members5/hotstocks

20. http://www.freeyellow.com:8080/members7/aaahotstocks

21. http://allstocks.com/copia/index.html

22. http://www.Quick-Picks.com

23. http://www.pennystockinsider.com

24. http://www.stockinsiders.com

25. http://www.dipwits.com/pennypick.htm

26. http://www.cybershops2000.com/picks.htm

27. http://www.ddinvestor.com

28. AOL

General Penny Stock Research Sites

1. http://www.dailystocks.com

    *this sites contains dozens of other useful links

2. http://www.freerealtime.com

3. http://www.tradepbs.com/pbscgi/hstqtetd?Symbol=

4. http://www.insidertrader.com/

5. http://www.investorlinks.com/

6. http://www.otcfn.com/bb/

7. http://www.otcbb.com/dynamic/

8. http://www.freedgar.com

9. http://www.stockjustice.com/

10. http://allstocks.com/copia/html/the_basics_of_otcbb.html

11. http://members.aol.com/jskowboy/index.html

12. http://www.otcbb.com/dynamic/tradingdata/top100list/top1
    00.htm

13. http://www.wallstreetnow.com/otcfinancialnetwork.htm

14. http://hh-club.com/

General Penny Stock Research Sites Continued...

15.   http://www.smallstocks.com/

16.   http://www.stock100.com

17.   http://www.litwick.com

18.   http://www.sec.gov/enforce/comctr.htm

19.   http://www.stockconsultant.com/consultnow

20.   http://www.pennystockland.com

21.   http://www.otcaccumulator.com

22.   http://www.sliceoflife.com/pennystocks/top100.asp

23.   http://www.webpennies.com

24.   http://www.pennystockpicks.com/links.html

Appendix B

Penny Stock Glossary

Ask: The price at which you can buy a stock.

Assets: Any possessions a company owns that have value.

Balance Sheet: A listing of all assets and liabilities for an individual or a business.

Balance Sheet Return: Sales/Price Ratio, Price/Book Ratio, Book/Share, Return on Equity, Profit Margin, and Reporting Date. These are all measures of company value and profitability.

Balance Sheet - Cash & Debt: Fiscal Year End, Quick Ratio, Debt/Equity Ratio, Current Ratio, and Cash/Share. Measures of the financial health of a company, particularly its assets and liabilities.

Basher: Someone who posts information in an effort to drive the price of a stock down.

Bid: The price at which you can sell your stock.

Block Trade: Usually, a trade of 10,000 shares or more. Penny stock block trades usually involve 100,000 shares or more.

Book/Share: The current fiscal year book value (or net equity for the corporation) per share of common stock.

Broker/Dealer: An agent who facilitates trades between a buyer and a seller and receives a commission for services. Dealers buy and sell for their own account and keep their own inventory of securities on which they can profit or incur losses. Most stock brokerage firms really act as brokers and dealers.

Buy-to-Cover: Purchasing stock to cover your short position. If you short a stock you must buy-to-cover in order to repay the brokerage the stock you borrowed from them.

Canceled Order: A buy or sell order that is canceled before it has been executed. A Limit Order can be can be canceled at any time as long as it has not been executed. A market order can only be canceled if the order is placed after the closing bell and is subsequently canceled before the opening bell of the following trading day.

Capital Stock: Amount of money or property contributed by stockholders to be used as the financial foundation for the corporation. It includes all classes of common and preferred stock.

Cash Flow: Net income plus depreciation and other non-cash charges.

Cash Market: A market in which security transactions occur within a few days of the trade date. Penny stocks trade in a cash market.

Class A/Class B Shares: Shares of stock issued by the same company but having some difference such as voting rights or a dividend preference.

Closing Price: Price of the stock at the close of trading for the day.

Commission: Fee charged by broker to execute your trade.

Common Shares: Represents the total number of common shares outstanding.

Common Stock: Stock representing partial ownership interest in a corporation. Ownership may also be shares with Preferred Stock, which has first claim on any dividends to be paid and, in the event of liquidation, to the distribution of the corporation's assets. Common stockholders assume the primary risk if business is poor, and realize greater gains in the event of success. They also elect the board of directors that controls the company.

Confirmation: A written notification from a broker to a client specifying the details of a stock transaction.

Current P/E Ratio: The ratio of current price divided by last two quarters earnings per share (EPS) plus next two estimated quarters EPS.

Current Year High & Low Prices: The highest and lowest price for a given stock during the current calendar year.

Current Ratio: A company's current assets divided by its current liabilities.

Date of Record: The date on which a shareholder must officially own shares in order to be entitled to a dividend. Most penny stocks do not pay out dividends however.

Day Order: The order will remain open for one trading day until it is executed or canceled. If the order is placed after market hours it will remain open for the next trading day. If it is placed during market hours it will remain open for the remainder of that trading day.

Deleted: A stock that is no longer included in The Nasdaq Stock Market.

Dividend: Distribution of earnings to shareholders, prorated by the class of security and paid in the form of money, stock, scrip, or, rarely, company products or property. The amount is decided by the Board of Directors and is usually paid quarterly. Most penny stocks do not pay out dividends.

Discount Broker: Brokerage firms that offer inexpensive transaction fees in lieu of not providing investment advice to clients. Most discount brokers offer online trading.

Dog: A stock that is not performing well.

Electronic Data Gathering, Analysis, and Retrieval EDGAR: An electronic system implemented by the SEC that is used by companies to transmit all documents required to be filed with the SEC in relation to corporate offerings and ongoing disclosure obligations. EDGAR became fully operational mid 1995.

Float: The number of shares a stock has available for trading purposes.

Gapper: The difference between the closing and opening prices for a stock on successive days. Stocks may gap up or down depending on the circumstances.

GTC: Good 'til canceled. A GTC order will remain open until it is executed or canceled, regardless of the number of trading days.

Held: A situation where a security is temporarily not available for trading and the Market Makers are not allowed to display quotes.

Hypster: Someone who posts information in an effort to boost the price of a stock.

Inside Market: The highest bid and the lowest offer prices among all competing Market Makers in a Nasdaq security, i.e., the best bid and offer prices.

Level 2 Trading: Type of service whereby an investor can view every market maker's bid/ask prices in real time and buy directly from the market maker of their choice.

Limit Order: An order in which you can set the maximum price you want to pay for your purchase, or a minimum price you will accept as seller.

Long: An investor who holds a stock for an extended period of time.

Limit Order: An order to buy or sell a stock at a customer-specified price.

Long Term Gain: A gain on the sale of a stock held six months or more and the profits are subject to the long term capital gains tax.

Market Order: This is an order that is executed immediately, at the best available price.

Market Makers: NASD member firms that represent a stock and compete with each other to buy and sell the stocks they represent. There numerous firms that act as OTCBB Market Makers. One of the major differences between the OTCBB and other major markets in the U.S. is the OTCBB's structure of competing Market Makers. Market Makers compete for customer orders by displaying different buy and sell quotes. Once an order is received, the Market Maker will immediately purchase for or sell from its own inventory.

Market Maker spread: The difference between the price at which a Market Maker is willing to buy a security and the price at which the firm is willing to sell it i.e., the difference between a Market Maker's bid and ask for a given security.

Market Order: An order to buy or sell a stated amount of a security at the current market rate.

Market Value: The market price; the price at which buyers and sellers trade similar items in an open marketplace. The current market price of a security as indicated by the latest trade recorded.

Material news: News released by a company that might be expected to affect the value of a company's stock or influence investors' decisions. Material news includes information regarding corporate events of an unusual nature, news of tender offers, unusually good or bad earnings reports, and a stock split or stock dividend.

MOMO Stock: Momentum mover. A risky investment strategy whereby a stock, usually unknown and thinly traded, is picked by investment clubs for intraday trading. Price fluctuations on these stocks can be very severe.

Most Active: Most active stocks usually by the number of shares traded per day.

National Association of Securities Dealers, Inc. NASD: The self regulatory organization of the securities industry responsible for the regulation of The Nasdaq Stock Market and the Over The Counter markets. The NASD operates under the authority granted it by the 1938 Maloney Act Amendment to the Securities Exchange Act of 1934.

Net Change: The difference between today's last trade and the previous day's last trade.

Net Worth: Surplus of assets over liabilities; what is owned free of debt.

Newbie: Someone who is a newcomer to stock investing; a novice stock trader.

Online Trading: The act of buying and selling securities electronically via computer. Most brokerage firms currently offer this service. Trading stocks online is usually less expensive than placing an order with a live broker.

Open order: An order to buy or sell a security that remains in effect until it is either canceled by the customer or executed.

Penny Stock: Name given to stocks that typically trade for less than $5. For the purposes of this book, penny stock refers to stocks traded on the OTCBB exchange for less than $1.

Pop: A quick gain in the price of a stock.

Previous Day's Close: The previous trading day's last reported trade.

Principal orders: Refers to activity by a broker/dealer when buying or selling for its own account and risk.

Pump & Dump: Risky trading practice often seen with penny stocks where a security quickly rises in value based on unsubstantiated claims and then subsequently falls in profit taking sell-offs.

Real-time trade reporting: A requirement imposed on Market Makers to report each trade immediately after completion of the transaction. Stocks traded on The Nasdaq Stock Market are subject to real time trade reporting within 90 seconds of execution.

Resistance Point: The point at which a stock tends to stall in its rise to new highs.

Retained Earnings: Net profits kept to accumulate in a business after dividends are paid.

Securities and Exchange Commission SEC: The federal agency created by the Securities Exchange Act of 1934 to administer that act and the Securities Act of 1933. The statutes administered by the SEC are designed to promote full public disclosure and protect the investing public against fraudulent and manipulative practices in the securities markets. Generally, most issues of securities offered in interstate commerce or through the mails must be registered with the SEC.

Selling Short: Selling short is the selling of a security that the seller does not own, or any sale that is completed by the delivery of a security borrowed by the seller. Short sellers assume the risk that they will be able to buy the stock at a less expensive price than the price at which they sold short.

Short Term Gain: The loss realized from the sale of stocks held six months or less.

Spread: The difference between the bid and the asking prices for a stock. The spread is commonly influenced by the size of the float, demand for the stock, and current trading activity.

Stock Dividend: Payment of a corporate dividend in the form of stock rather than cash. The stock dividend may be additional shares in the company, or it may be shares in a subsidiary being spun off to shareholders. Stock dividends are often used to conserve cash needed to operate the business. Unlike a cash dividend, stock dividend are not taxed until sold. Most penny stocks do not have a stock dividend payment.

Stock symbol: A unique four- or five-letter symbol assigned to an OTCBB security. Definitions of fifth symbols can be found in Chapter 2 FAQ.

Stop: This is an order that converts to a market order once the stock trades at the stop price you have specified.

Stop Limit: This is an order that combines both the stop and limit order, in that once the stop price is activated your order can be executed up to your limit price. However, in a fast moving market, your trade may not be executed if the price goes past your limit.

Subpenny: Stocks that trade at one cent or lower on a daily basis.

Tanking: When a stock loses its value very quickly.

Ten-K Report (10K): Annual report that all companies must file with the Securities and Exchange Comission (SEC). This report contains vital company information such as financial statements, pending lawsuits against the company, company history, and future plans.

Today's High: The intra-day high trading price.

Today's Low: The intra-day low trading price.

Trading halt: The temporary suspension of trading in a OTCBB. Only the SEC has authority to halt trading on a OTBB security.

Volume: Total number of shares traded.

Yield: A return on an investor's capital investment.

Appendix C

Penny Stocks Worth Looking At

From personal experience, I know that finding potential penny stock investments can be challenging. For many investors the only penny stocks they are exposed to come from the penny stock newsletters and pick sites. While these are excellent sources of information, they only expose a fraction of the thousands of penny stocks out there. The following is a list that contains many leaders of the penny stock market. Of course, the hot penny stocks will change over time, but this list should provide you with a good starting point to jump into the world of penny stock investing. Also included in this list are a many relatively unknown penny and subpenny securities. Who knows, the next big winner might be residing on this very list!

Note: Due to the ever-changing nature of the penny stock world, some of the companies on this list may have changed symbols, merged with other companies, or disappeared from the face of the earth. To get a complete list of all companies that trade on the OTCBB, go to http://www.otcbb.com and check out "stock summaries" on the market statistics page. This list is gargantuan, but it will provide you with the symbols of ever security traded on the OTCBB market.

A

ABRG	Ambra Resources Group, Inc.
ACTB	Action Sports International, Inc.
ADGIE	American Diversified Group, Inc.
ADVR	Advanced Viral Research Corp.
AGCR	Agiss Corporation
AIGI	Adair International Oil and Gas, Inc.
APPI	Advanced Plant Pharmaceuticals
AQCI	Aquatic Cellulose International Corp.
AREE	Arete Industries, Inc.
ARET	Ameriresourse Technologies, Inc.
ARTM	American Nortel Communications
AUMY	Aunt Myras, Inc.

B

BIBNE	BIB.net Corp.
BICO	Biocontrol Tech, Inc.
BISN	Biosonics, Inc.
BNEZ	Ben Ezra Weinstein & Co.
BNTI	Braintech, Inc.
BODY	Bio-Dyne Corp.
BOOK	Village Green Bookstores, Inc.
BPMD	Boston Pacific Medical, Inc.
BRZS	Brazos Sportswear, Inc.
BUKS	Butler National Corporation
BSBI	Big Smith Brands, Inc.
BYIT	Household Direct.com

C

CASG	Canadian Aerospace International, Inc.
CATV	Channel America Broadcast, Inc.
CAYC	Caye Chappel, Inc.
CCGR	Collectible Concepts Groups, Inc.
CDNO	Cons Capital North America, Inc.
CHES	Chester Holdings, LTD.
CHOP	Tmanglobal.com, Inc.
CHUR	Churchill Technologies
CISI	CIS.com, Inc.
CLNI	Clinicorp, Inc.
CMLK	CML Group, Inc.
CMMI	Consolidated Medical Management, Inc.
CODD	Coded Communication Corp.
CYYSQ	Cityscape Financial Corp.

D

DACQ	Dynamic American Corp
DANS	Danskin, Inc.
DATV	Datatrend Services, Inc.
DCCC	DCCC
DGIX	Dyna Group International
DIET	Surequest Systems, Inc.
DIGG	Digital Gas, Inc.
DLNZ	D-Lanz Development Group, Inc.
DMEC	Diamond Entertainment Corp.
DREV	Dragon environmental Corp.
DRYD	Dryden Inds.
DYGN	Dynagen, Inc.
DCGR	DCGR International Holdings, Inc.

E

EJTX	Energetics, Inc.
ENZH	Enzymes American Holding Corp.
EPEA	E-Prime Aerospace Corp.
EPUR	Enviropur Waste
EREX	E-Rex, Inc.
ESEX	Essex Corp.
ETKA	Ethika Corp.
EUGS	Eurogas, Inc.
EUTO	Eutro Group Holding, Inc.
EVDS	Environmental Digital Services, Inc.
EVSA	Envirosafe Corp.
EZZZ	Easy Access International, Inc.

F

FASC	First American Scientific Corp.
FCCX	First Central Financial Corp.
FFLM	First Films
FIXN	Famous Fixins, Inc.
FLOS	Dental Services of America
FNET	Futurenet, Inc.
FOCS	Fiberchem, Inc.
FONX	Fonix Corp.
FRRF	FRRF
FRXX	Forecross Corp.
FTCFQ	Freuhauf Trailer Corp.
FWAT	Flexwatt Corp.

G

GAAY	Triangle Broadcasting Co., Inc. New
GAMZ	Gamecom, Inc.
GBFE	Golden Books Family Entertainment
GOBO	Global Boulevard International, Inc.
GOTKQ	Gotech Communications, Inc.
GRAR	Great American Recreation, Inc.
GSIC	General Store International, Inc.
GSIT	Ginsite Materials, Inc.
GTEC	Grip Technologies
GTST	Global Telecomm Solutions, Inc.
GUSH	Fountain Oil, Inc.
GWTS	Gateways to Space Entertainment
GZON	Graphix Zone, Inc.

H

HABE	Haber
HARD	Novex Systems International, Inc.
HARR	Harrison Digicom, Inc.
HAYZQ	Hayes Corp.
HDST	Bullseye Marketing Corp.
HICC	Harbour Intermodal, Inc.
HIVX	Bioquest, Inc.
HOPR	Holly Holdings, Inc.
HTNZ	Hollywood Trendz
HRNT	H&R Enterprises
HVAR	Havanna Republic
HYPD	Hyperdynamics Corp.
HZOG	Herzog International Holdings, Inc.

I

IABS	International Absorbents, Inc.
IDCN	Indocan Resources, Inc.
IFUE	International Fuel, Inc.
IGTN	Image Guided Technologies, Inc.
IINN	International Internet, Inc.
IMTI	Imagyn Medical Techs, Inc.
IMTKA	Information Management Tech.
INCE	Intercell Corp New
INII	I Net, Inc.
ININ	International Industries, Inc.
INNN	Interactive Network, Inc.
INTE	Industrial Technologies, Inc.
IPAK	Integrated Package Assembly Corp.
IRCE	Interline Resources Corp.
ISDN	Globalnet Systems Ltd.
ISSS	Integrated Spatial Information Solutions
ITEK	International Tourist Entertainment Corp.
IVOC	IVOICE.com, Inc.
IWAX	International Wellness Association

J

JACC	Jayhawk Acceptance Corp.
JACK	Golden Bear Golf
JAHI	Jordan American Holdings, Inc.
JAWS	Great White Marine Recreation
JAWZ	Jaws Technologies, Inc.
JAXI	Jax International, Inc.
JBRD	J-Bird, Inc.
JEMG	Jagged Edge Mountain Gear
JNNE	Jones Naughton Entertainment, Inc.
JOES	Eat at Joe's, Inc.

JRSE	Jacobson Resonance Enterprises
JSUB	Jreck Subs Group, Inc.
JUST	Just Toys

K

KAHI	Kaire Holdings, Inc.
KANA	Kanakaris Communications
KBIZ	Knowledgebroker, Inc.
KESE	Keystone Energy Sevices, Inc.
KICK	Master Glazier's Karate International
KIDM	Kid's Mart
KISS	Kismit Energy Corp.
KMGG	Kaleidoscope Media Group, Inc.
KNET	Kinetiks Com, Inc.
KNII	Knight Industries, Inc.
KRUZ	Europa Cruises
KTAX	Kaye Kotts Associates, Inc.
KTNX	Kentex Energy, Inc.
KWTL	KWT Ltd.

L

LAKO	Lakota Energy, Inc.
LAZT	Lasertech International, Inc.
LDSR	Landstar, Inc.
LEDS	Lucas Educational Systems, Inc.
LGOV	Largo Vista Group LTD
LILM	LIL Mark, Inc.
LKON	Linkon Corp.
LLOG	Lincoln Logs
LMAR	Lamaur Corp.
LNSH	Lionshare Group, Inc.
LOCH	Loch Harris, Inc.
LONG	Integral Health, Inc.

LONE	Lifeone, Inc.
LOTS	Lot$ Off Corp.
LTTO	Lotto World, Inc.
LVFIQ	Levitz Furniture

M

MACH	Mach One Corp.
MAMH	Mamatech Corp.
MBST	Microbest, Inc.
MDHM	Medinah Mining, Inc.
MEMO	Voice It Worldwide, Inc.
MGTK	Magnesium Technologies, Inc.
MLTI	Medical Laser Technologies, Inc.
MMDI	MRI Medical Diagnostics
MMMP	Mobile Multimedia Productions
MNLT	Monalta Resources International
MPTV	MPTV, Inc.
MOOR	Chadmore Wireless Group, Inc.
MOLY	Worldwide Petromoly, Inc.
MRAY	Murray Utd. Dev. Corp.
MRTI	Metal Recovery Technologies, Inc.
MTCH	Meditech Pharmaceuticals
MTLL	Mactell Corp.
MVEE	1st Miracle Group, Inc.

N

NALF	NAL Financial Group, Inc.
NBMX	National Boston Medical
NCTI	NCT Group, Inc.
NHLT	National Health & Safety
NIAR	North American Resorts, Inc. New
NIGI	Nigi
NNUP	Nocopi Technologies, Inc.

NPEC	NP Energy Corp. New
NRMM	Netrom, Inc.
NSKY	New Sky Communications, Inc.
NUKE	Rhombic Corp.
NUOA	Nuoasis Resorts, Inc.
NUTK	Nutek, Inc.
NVID	Nvid Interational, Inc.
NWAV	North Wave Comm. Corp.
NYBS	New York Bagel Enterprises, Inc.
NYRR	New York Regional Rail Corp.

O

OAIS	Oasis Resorts International
OBTY	Orbit Technologies, Inc.
ODDS	Sport of Kings, Inc.
ODSA	Odessa Foods International, Inc.
OKOK	Oklahoma Energy Corp.
OLEX	Oilex, Inc.
OMDA	O Media, Inc.
ONSE	Onsite Energy Corp.
ONTV	LA Group, Inc.
OPAL	Opal Technologies, Inc.
OPIX	Odyssey Pictures Corp.
ORCA	Orca technologies, Inc.
OZON	Cyclopss Corp.

P

PABN	Pan American BanCorp
PAMM	Pacificamerican Money Center, Inc.
PAPO	Pangea Petroleum Corp.
PARR	Bullet Sports International, Inc.
PAYP	Pay Pop, Inc.
PCBM	Pinnacle Business Management, Inc.

PEPI	Piezo Electric Products
PHLB	Pharmaceutical Labs
PICK	Pick Communications Corp.
PINC	Planet City Corp.
PLEX	PLEX
PLRP	Pacel Corp.
PNDA	Panda Project, Inc.
POFM	Pacesetter Ostrich Farm, Inc.
POKR	Casino Airlink, Inc.
PPMC	Purchase Point Media Corp.
PREV	Prevenco, Inc.
PRXX	Praxis Pharmaceuticals, Inc.
PWDR	Power Direct, Inc.
PWSP	Power Spectra

Q

QGRP	Quartz Group, Inc.
QIXXF	Quest International Resources Corp.
QPIX	Quick Pix, Inc.
QPRC	Quest Products Corp.
QSTI	Questec Imaging, Inc.
QTNT	Quick Tent
QTTM	Quantitative Methods Corp.
QUAD	Quad
QUIL	Quill Industries, Inc.
QUOB	Queryobject Systems

R

RAACQ	Reliance Acceptance Group, Inc.
RADO	Alliance Broadcasting Group
RCVI	Rock City Ventures, Inc.
RDOX	Redox Technology Corp.
REDI	Reddi Brake Supply Corp.
REPR	Repro Med Systems
RDMG	RDM Sports Group, Inc.
RGEQ	Rgeq
RIHI	Ranes International Holdings, Inc.
RNET	RNETHEALTH.com
RPIN	Rotary Power International, Inc.
RPIX	Royal Pictures, Inc.
RTII	RTI, Inc.
RTTL	Rattlesnake Holding Co., Inc.

S

SATKQ	Substance Abuse Technologies
SENS	Sentex Sensing Technologies, Inc.
SETO	Seto Holdings, Inc.
SFAD	Safe Technologies International, Inc.
SHCC	Saratoga International Holdings Corp.
SHMN	Shaman Pharm, Inc.
SHRO	Sports Heroes, Inc.
SITE	Site Technologies, Inc.
SKYS	Sky Scientific, Inc.
SLCTY	Select Software Tools PLC
SNTVQ	Sun Television and Appliance
SNTS	Sani-Tech Industries, Inc.
SOLU	Wireless Data Solutions, Inc.
SPAZ	Spatializer Audio Labs, Inc.
SPTS	Sports Media, Inc.

SRAN	Simtek Corp.
SSTH	Scott Science and Technology, Inc.
STDS	Scottsdale Scientific, Inc.
STEL	S.A. Telecommunications
STGI	Steroidogenesis Inhibitors International
STLR	Star Technologies, Inc.
STRU	Struthers, Inc.
SUBM	Submicron Systems Corp.
SWSI	SWSI, Inc.
SXXC	Source Energy Group
SYCR	Syncrony's Softcorp
SYEP	Soy Environmental Products

T

TBOP	Topper's Brick Oven Pizza
TEXN	21st Century Technologies
TITT	Titan Technologies
TMMI	TMM, Inc. New
TNRG	Tianrong Building Materials Holdings LTD
TOPZ	Topaz Group, Inc.
TPIE	TPI Enterprises
TREY	Treasury International, Inc.
TRKR	Tracker Corp. of America
TSIG	Teleservices International, Inc.
TSIS	Interactive Telesis, Inc.
TTFC	Telefficiency Holding Corp.
TTRIF	Thermo Tech, Inc.
TUBY	Tubby's, Inc.
TVIN	TVI
TXAG	Texas American Group, Inc.
TXCI	Totalaxcess.com, Inc.
TXMC	Tirex Corp.

U

UAMY	United States Antimony Corp.
UCIA	UCI Medical Affiliates, Inc.
UFLY	Seair Corp.
UNDY	UniDyn Corp.
USAV	Costplusfive.com, Inc.
USCI	Unistat, Inc.
USCM	USCI, Inc.
USPS	Usps
USVO	USA Video Interactive Corp.
UVTF	Universal Turf

V

VALH	Value Holdings, Inc.
VCAH	Vencap Holdings, Inc.
VDOT	Virtualsellers.com, Inc.
VHSN	VHS Network, Inc.
VIKG	Viking Resources International, Inc
VINS	Vins
VIRT	Virtual Reality Networks
VLVT	Veltex Corp.
VPTI	Voice Powered Technologies Intl, Inc.
VRDE	Veridien Corp.
VRFT	Vitafort International Corp.
VSTI	Versus Technology, Inc.
VTEH	Venture Tech, Inc.
VYGP	Voyager RP USA Brazil Ltd

W

WADE	Wade Cook Financial Corp.
WAMA	Watermarc Food Management Co.
WASP	Wasatch Pharmaceutical
WAXX	Waxman Industries, Inc
WINW	World Internetworks, Inc
WNCR	Winchester Mining Corp.
WOOD	Madera International, Inc.
WOWS	Wowstores.com, Inc.
WPOG	Pease Oil & Gas Co.
WPUR	Waterpur International, Inc.
WRKE	Work Recovery, Inc.
WSYS	Westergaard.com, Inc
WTER	Water Chef
WVIS	World Vision Holdings, Inc.
WWAT	World Water Corp.
WWDE	World Wide Equipment Corp.
WWLI	White Wing Labs
WYOM	Wyom
WZTC	Wiz Technology, Inc.

X

XCHG	Telpac Industries, Inc.
XCLU	Exclusive Cruises and Resorts
XENOW	Xenometrics, Inc.
XNSR	Xensor Corp.
XPIE	Coastal Foods, Inc.
XPLA	Explorer S A
XSEL	Solar Energy Ltd.
XSYS	XSYS Technologies, Inc.
XTIC	Xi Tec, Inc.
XYVI	Xyvision, Inc.

Y

YAAKA	Yaaka
YARC	Yarc Systems Corporation, Inc.
YESS	Yes! Entertainment Group
YRLS	Coomtec International, Inc.
YSCO	Yes Clothing Co., Inc.

Z

ZARAF	Zarara Oil & Gas Ltd.
ZERO	Save the World Air, Inc.
ZETA	Zeta Corp.
ZETHQ	Zenith Electronics
ZITI	Ziti
ZNIC	Znic
ZNRG	Zydeco Energy, Inc.
ZSON	Sonic Systems Corp.
ZULU	Zulu Tek, Inc.
ZYCN	Zycom, Inc.

Afterword

Investing in penny stocks can be a thoroughly enjoyable and rewarding experience. I have made much more money investing in penny stocks than I have with my NYSE and Nasdaq investments. I hope that you have found the information presented in this book both informative and helpful. I wish you the best of luck and hope that you can catch one of those 9000% one-day wonders like KIDM! Please let me know what you think of the book and if there is something you would like to see differently in future editions.

Good Luck!

Danny Holtzclaw

Index

goldrush, 20

H

housing starts, 42
Hypsters, 8, 35, 62, 93, 95, 96

I

IBM, 20
IGHS, 18
interest rates, 42
internet, 10, 12, 14, 16, 17, 19, 21, 29, 34, 58, 89, 93

K

KIDM, 68, 140

L

Lawsuit, 98
limit order, 25, 28, 34, 62, 72, 92, 131
links, 43
longs, 93, 94, 95
lottery, 18
lotto, 11

M

mailing lists, 46, 47
margin, 25
market, 11
market maker, 15, 25, 127
market makers, 10, 15, 22, 24, 25, 26, 27, 34, 49, 59, 62, 65, 84, 85, 92, 94
market order, 10, 25, 27, 34, 72, 124, 131
message board, 21
message boards, 26, 34, 43, 46, 99
Microsoft, 20
MM, 22, 24, 25, 26, 27, 104
momentum, 42
MOMO, 8, 26, 71, 72, 73, 74, 128
MPTV, 20, 141
mutual funds, 13

Notes

Notes

Notes

<u>Re-Order Form</u>

- **Name:** _____

- **Address:**_____

  _____

  _____

- **Price:**   **$15.95 (Customer Loyalty Discount)**
- **Shipping:**
    USA and Canada: **$4.00**
    INT'L: **$10.00**
- **Tax:**
    Texas residents please add 8.25% sales tax ($1.48)

- **Please send check or money order for $15.95 plus shipping:**

    Greek Financial Services
    114 Rose Way
    Salado, TX 76571

- **Allow 7-10 days for delivery, longer for Int'l orders.**

Contact us: gfs@ragingbull.com